Advance Praise for *How to* ...

"No one thinks, unpacks, illumines, and reckons with horror, both personal and pop cultural, quite the way Peter Counter does. *How to Restore a Timeline* is a brilliant, humorous, heartbreaking examination of how certain events break our lives apart, and what we do with the pieces."
—John Hodgman, bestselling author of *Medallion Status: True Stories from Secret Rooms* and *Vacationland: True Stories from Painful Beaches*

"Beautifully written, genuinely moving, and totally inventive. Intelligent and unflinching. A haunting rumination on trauma, memory, survival, media, and violence. Essential reading."
—Rachel Harrison, bestselling author of *Cackle* and *Such Sharp Teeth*

"Once I started Peter Counter's *How to Restore a Timeline*, I couldn't put it down. There is such beauty, intelligence, and deftness that infuses not only each essay in this incredible book, but each sentence, each word. Counter takes us by the hand and leads us through his own trauma-disrupted timeline, and in so doing, gives us the maps and schematics by which we can approach—and maybe even restore—our own. This is a book to hold close in our most difficult moments—and to return to when those difficult moments come crashing unexpectedly back."
—Alicia Elliott, author of *A Mind Spread Out on the Ground*

"In exploring his own personal traumas, Peter Counter's incisive writing leaves behind an exit wound of its own. Every essay is a piece of pop culture shrapnel that fractures in the reader's mind. You will heal, but you'll carry the scars of this profound collection forever."
—Clay McLeod Chapman, author of *Ghost Eaters*

"Suffused with warmth and humour yet unsparing in its honesty, Peter Counter's genre-defying new work challenges us to explore the unturned pages and unshared stories in our own lives and consider how we could take power over them and change them for the better."

—David Demchuk, author of *The Bone Mother* and *RED X*

"Peter Counter is our guide through the labyrinth, the string he provides anchoring each tailored diversion into pop culture. Hold tight to that thread as these essays converge, revealing a book built to house our collective hauntings, its alcoves overflowing with insight into the visceral demands of memory."

—Andrew F. Sullivan, author of *The Marigold*
and *The Handyman Method*

"Exhilarating. A work of intellectually rigorous cultural criticism that reads like a thriller. I was hooked from the very first page."

—Melissa Maerz, author of *Alright, Alright, Alright:*
The Oral History of Richard Linklater's Dazed and Confused

"The way Peter Counter writes about trauma is an extraordinary thing. He explores violence and its consequences, the compulsive revisions and relivings and ripple effects, with a merciless, loving specificity. In a book so gore-soaked and anguished, Counter manages something rare: *How to Restore a Timeline* is as kind as it is brutal. This book's hands are bloody, but they are holding yours."

—Natalie Zina Walschots, author of *Hench*

HOW TO RESTORE A TIMELINE

HOW TO RESTORE A TIMELINE

ON VIOLENCE AND MEMORY

PETER COUNTER

ANANSI

Published in Canada in 2023 and the USA in 2023 by House of Anansi Press Inc.
houseofanansi.com

House of Anansi Press is committed to protecting our natural environment. This book is made of material from well-managed FSC®-certified forests, recycled materials, and other controlled sources.

House of Anansi Press is a Global Certified Accessible™ (GCA by Benetech) publisher. The ebook version of this book meets stringent accessibility standards and is available to readers with print disabilities.

27 26 25 24 23   1 2 3 4 5

Library and Archives Canada Cataloguing in Publication

Title: How to restore a timeline : on violence and memory / Peter Counter.
Names: Counter, Peter, 1987- author.
Description: Includes bibliographical references.
Identifiers: Canadiana (print) 2023044301X | Canadiana (ebook) 20230443052 |
ISBN 9781487011994 (softcover) | ISBN 9781487012007 (EPUB)
Subjects: LCSH: Counter, Peter, 1987——Mental health. | LCSH: Post-traumatic stress disorder—Biography. | LCGFT: Autobiographies.
Classification: LCC RC552.P67 C685 2023 | DDC 616.85/210092—dc23

Cover design: Greg Tabor
Text design and typesetting: Lucia Kim

House of Anansi Press is grateful for the privilege to work on and create from the Traditional Territory of many Nations, including the Anishinabeg, the Wendat, and the Haudenosaunee, as well as the Treaty Lands of the Mississaugas of the Credit.

With the participation of the Government of Canada
Avec la participation du gouvernement du Canada | Canadä

We acknowledge for their financial support of our publishing program the Canada Council for the Arts, the Ontario Arts Council, and the Government of Canada.

Printed and bound in Canada

For Dad.
For Mom.
For Nick.
For Emma.

The names and identifying details of people mentioned herein have been changed to protect their privacy. The exceptions are public figures, my dearest friends, and my family. If any of you remember the events of this book differently: I believe you.

The timeline contains multitudes.

CONTENTS

TRIGGER WARNINGS AND SPOILER ALERTS

Spoiler Alert
The next section is a trigger warning, which is a type of spoiler. A trigger is a specific detail the audience hasn't yet encountered, like the gun that will be fired later in this essay. Somewhat paradoxically, that is also the definition of a spoiler. I can't give you the information you need to be safe without ruining the surprises contained in this book. Would you rather be safe or entertained? Don't answer that. This essay makes both outcomes impossible. Apologies in advance.

Trigger Warning
This book contains detailed descriptions of gun violence, self-harm, and suicidal ideation, as well as meticulous examinations of PTSD and bipolar II symptoms, including flashbacks, hypervigilance, hypomania, and depression. If spoilers for media and entertainment tend to ruin your day,

there are plenty of those too. The essays in here describe certain key plot points and aesthetic details for *The Shining*, *Silent Hill 2*, *The Green Knight*, *A Muppet Christmas Carol*, *Seinfeld*, Neil Gaiman's *Whatever Happened to the Caped Crusader?*, most live-action Batman movies, *Kill Bill*, *Oldboy*, and *Tai Chi Master*.

I'm not entirely sure you can spoil music, but just in case, the discography of Linkin Park is in here, and Coldplay's fourth record, along with a Cat Stevens best-of album issued by Universal Records and David Bowie's *Diamond Dogs*. I am going to make a joke about Jeb Bush's 2015 Republican primary campaign, deconstruct *The Ring* and its various adaptations, evoke the ending of *Final Fantasy VIII*, mention *Uncharted 2*, and unravel the byzantine threads of *Metal Gear Solid V: The Phantom Pain*. The plot is laid out for *Hades*, *Fringe*, *Back to the Future*, and *Search Party*, and important details from the following media will be described to help evoke pathos and illustrate abstract emotional concepts: *Slaughterhouse-Five*, *Taskmaster*, *Dragon Ball Z*, *Twin Peaks*, *Nope*, *Battlestar Galactica*, and a YouTube video titled "Glock Cleaning ASMR for INSTANT relaxation | Gun Sounds for sleep."

As far as spoilers go, that might already be too much. The very suggestion that something might be spoilable to sensitive audiences reveals that there are plot details worth hiding. "You have to go in knowing as little as possible," is what I tell my brother, Nick—who has more than once slandered my name as a serial spoiler—whenever I recommend a movie, show, game, or book. Meanwhile, the detail in the above paragraphs is not nearly enough information to adequately warn survivors of trauma that their symptoms might be triggered by the words printed on these pages. Sure, there's gun violence, but is it the kind I find entertaining? Or will it make me fall to the floor in the throes of a violent memory wave?

Perhaps you are starting to see my conundrum.

Spoiler Alert

This subsection describes the core anecdotal details contained in this essay collection. You might not expect an essay collection to have a plot, but this one comes close. The memoir pieces herein all concern, in one way or another, the events of December 27, 2006. That date is etched with acid on the concrete of every one of my memories. Events that happened before and after that date are all warped by its gravity, distorted and claimed as misshapen satellites orbiting this worst day of my life. The violence starts now.

My parents took Nick and I on a family cruise for Christmas. I was nineteen and in theatre school, and growing into my identity as a young adult with bipolar II. Five days into the cruise, on December 27, we moored in Limon, Costa Rica. Nick and my mom went on a rainforest zipline excursion. Left to our own devices, Dad and I decided to explore the town on foot, sticking to the safe places indicated on the map handed out by the ship staff. We strolled through the market set up at the port—a merchant bazaar of souvenir tables and barbeque grills sheltered from the morning rain by a canopy of blue tarps. Traipsing through the town proper, the bars and tourist traps quickly gave way to rows of appliance stores and people sleeping on the streets.

No place for a couple of aimless white tourists. We turned around, but on our way back to the ship we spied a wooden pier just beyond a shady park across from the municipal hall. In my memory, I feel a sense of dread when we choose to look out at the ocean instead of returning to the boat. But that's just dramatic irony. I've seen how this ends.

Gazing over the pier's railing at a turbulent ocean, we were approached by a man.

"I think this guy is gonna try to sell us something," I said.

"No," said Dad.

The stranger blocked our escape and pulled out a revolver. It was blue with a brown handle and I thought it was a toy. He waved it at us, asking for money. But we'd left our cash on the ship. The man became more aggressive and my dad snapped. He began to kick at the gunman's hand with the rage of a challenged father. The man turned to flee and—*POP*.

Dad collapsed on the pier. I never saw the stranger again.

Trigger Warning

Humidity, running, martial arts, time travel, Christmas, secrets, religion, blood of the father, formal dinners, drug use, cognitive behavioural therapy, desperate hugs, ocean water, razor blades and a leather belt, theatre school. This is not a comprehensive list. It can't be. Seventeen years after that mind-rending gunshot, I still don't have a full inventory of my own personal triggers, and I can't possibly anticipate yours. But I want to.

One drizzly autumn day, many years after the shooting, I took what could be argued as too many psychedelic drugs all at once. I had two partners on this trip, and we were not adequately prepared for what was going to happen next. We dosed ourselves, taking only two pieces of advice for guidance: remember that the most intense part is behind you, and don't look in the mirror.

One of my companions became nonverbal save for the occasional alarming query ("What is currency?" and later, "What is a movie?") and frequent ominous realization ("Uh-oh …"). The other companion ran upstairs and hid in bed, convinced that taking the drugs was a mistake. I imagined my blood as paisley-patterned as it coursed through my veins, rushed to my brain's well-travelled trauma centres, and activated my fight-or-flight response. I ran up and down the stairs, juggling my fellow travellers' near-crisis emotional needs, keeping them safe, putting on a calm face and telling them over and over that I was just a little further ahead of them on our journey and it was going to get better for them very soon. The most intense part is behind us.

"When you get to where I am, and you're almost there," I said to the bed-person who seemed to have become one with the writhing lavender sheets, "you'll feel better."

Back downstairs, I turned on the smart TV in the living room, which displayed a digital clock in front of beautiful stock images of landscapes. I told the couch-person that every time the numbers increased we would be one step closer to the other side. We waited and our bodies warped— big torsos, little heads, celestial locks of golden hair. The numbers didn't change. Our groovy nightmare slipped out of bounds, time-wise.

"Just watch them move," I said, doubling down. "These drugs are supposed to feel good."

"Uh-oh..."

I'm telling you this story because you and I are on a journey together and I want you to be safe. I will be running
up and down the proverbial stairs, reassuring you. But as
the saying goes, you can't save a person drowning if you're
sinking in the same water. That said, trust me: I've sunk a
little deeper, and it's all right down here. Reading is supposed
to feel good.

Spoiler Alert

I'm about to tell you that my dad survived his shooting.
I helped carry him to safety. Staunching the blood pouring
from his chest wound with my green hoodie, I slung his arm
over my shoulders and dragged him through the streets like
we were competing in a high-stakes father-and-son three-
legged race. I dropped him a few times. I prayed once. At
some point I had to fight off a regiment of local paramed-
ics because no one on the ship knew where we were, and
I worried that if Dad died in a Costa Rican hospital I'd be
left stranded.

Three morning drinkers emerged from a shady TV-lit bar
and helped me. We carried Dad to the customs checkpoint
ahead of the ship, where I had to fish my now-unconscious
father's passport out of his shorts. Thinking of this, I am still
overcome with the strange intimacy of sightlessly feeling
around in his netted swim trunks pockets. The soft lining,
the heat—for me, touch is a rare type of sense memory.

More strangers ran to me, helping to rush Dad's body the
rest of the way to the gargantuan white ship. Inside the boat,
Dad cycled between lucidity and unconsciousness while the

medical officer stitched him up. He was deemed well enough to accompany me and a ship's representative on a tour of the police station where we failed to pick the assailant out of a lineup, and the courthouse where Dad and I had our statements taken. We made it back to the ship before Nick and Mom, and our vacation continued. We ended the day drinking under a sunset on the ship's Lido Deck, where the party never ends.

My dad survived his shooting.

That's it. The plot of my life's big story has been revealed. But there is more detail, and each brushstroke of memory is both a trigger and a spoiler. Disclosure fails to account for the data overload of human experience, and that's what we're dealing with here. It's the minutiae of a story that makes you shake with residual trauma. The memories you avoid replaying and the songs you put on repeat. The recurring dreams you dread or the films you rewatch. This is the realm of memory and surprise—welcome or intrusive, connected all the same.

After I was traumatized, I slunk away into a cave of media overload. I spent all my money on DVD box sets of TV shows I picked up on sale at Future Shop and ten-dollar CDs from HMV. Ever since I was four, when my dad sat me down in front of a small television set with the channel turned to *Teenage Mutant Ninja Turtles*, I've been obsessed with entertainment media. But this was different. I slipped through a crack and sank in an aquifer of flashing lights and noise and running director commentary tracks. At the time, I barely realized my behaviour had changed. Watching *Lost* and *Battlestar Galactica* until I knew every episode by number and title seemed perfectly reasonable. Waking up to the saturated glow of a *Simpsons* DVD menu and hitting "play all" so I could fall back to sleep was a nightly ritual. Giant over-ear Sony headphones were a perpetual part of my wardrobe, hanging around my neck like a collar when they weren't noise-cancelling the world around me.

I didn't feel like I was drowning. It wasn't until two years after the shooting, while attending a university lecture for a course called Modes of Fantasy, that I felt the need to gasp for air. In an attempt to make a point about how little young people read, the professor asked us to tally how much screen time we logged in a week.

"I hope this one is an error," he said, compiling the stats behind his lectern, ruffled by my reported ninety weekly hours of TV and film. "Someone here either needs math tutoring or is in serious trouble."

He was probably right on both counts. Less than six months later, I suffered a nervous breakdown and found myself in therapy. I needed someone outside the water to throw me a life preserver and pull me to safety, but I had been looking for salvation in a reflection. That's what media is, after all: a mirror. It fits us into frame and, at its best, shows us narratives and themes we can use to better understand the context of our pain, laughter, love, disgust, sorrow, and joy. The Technicolor looking glass doesn't contain answers, but it can trigger catharsis. Not through some grand plot twist or surprise reveal, but through that intimate connection we make with the person we see in the reflecting surface. We stare into the medium and find an echo of ourselves open to analysis, even when we've already seen this episode, read this book, played this level, stared at this clock on the smart TV. This time it might feel different, because you're different.

No one can protect you from yourself but you. When it comes to triggers and spoilers, we walk the path alone, guided by boldfaced warnings that can't possibly protect us from what's coming up next after the break. Viewer discretion is advised.

WAITING FOR THE RED GIANT

THE CORONAVIRUS DIDN'T END the world, and I know that because I'm driving to visit my parents at their home in the Rideau Lakes region of Ontario. It's been nearly six hundred days since I saw them last, and I've become a newly vaccinated road warrior because that's what you do in a post-apocalyptic narrative.

The best post-apocalypse stories are road stories. Movies like *Mad Max: Fury Road*, video games like *Fallout 3* or *The Last of Us* (which was adapted into a record-breaking HBO series)—they are wasteland odysseys fuelled by the morbid curiosity of what happened to the rest of the world. The game *The Last of Us* takes you from Boston to Salt Lake City via Pittsburgh, with each stop providing another opportunity to show you overgrown and flooded municipal infrastructure, frozen after 2013 when a pandemic of fungus zombies levelled society. When I played *Fallout 3* for the first time, I made an avatar in my image and went sightseeing through the nuked corpse of Washington, D.C., using a real-life map to find in-game locations like the Lincoln Memorial and the Capitol Building.

Of course, in making these trips and experiencing these stories, we have to acknowledge the ten-megaton glowing elephant in the room: post-apocalypse narratives aren't really about what happens after the world ends. We don't know how to tell stories that take place after the epilogue. They're really stories about survival, fantasies about freedom from social structure.

Navigating my digital self through *Fallout 3*'s collapsed subways and mutant-infested streets while trying to find a clear path to the White House, I tune the radio on my in-game smart watch to Three Dog—a radio DJ who spins oldies like Danny Kaye and the Andrews Sisters, complete with vinyl crackle. In addition to providing a tour of destroyed cities, the *Fallout* series is famous for its 1950s nostalgia. By evoking a time far in our own past, the game emotionally strings the player between two fantasies: a cleaned-up, idealized life that came before us, and a freer life that will come after social collapse. That's the escapism of post-apocalyptic fiction: if only the world would end, we'd be free to improve our lives.

My own road trip is punctuated by signs declaring the impossibility of entering New York State from the highway. I ask my phone to play "Five Years" by David Bowie and a robot voice informs me that's also impossible. Something about connectivity problems. Forced to scan the airwaves for tunes, I find a station broadcasting a klaxon alarm. It blares so loud, like a dial tone through a distortion pedal, I feel it in my teeth. I let it play until the unmistakable voice of a classic rock radio DJ interrupts.

"This is a test of the emergency broadcast system," he says in the same cadence I imagine he uses to announce the next track in a thirty-minute no-ads rock ride. "In a real emergency, this alarm will be accompanied by further instructions."

The mechanical shrieking sounds again.

Nothing confirms survival like an alarm test. Time to prepare for what's coming next. Time to reflect on what happened before. It's not over yet.

THREE WEEKS BEFORE I was born, Johnny Carson helped cancel the apocalypse. The Mayan long-form calendar, as interpreted by New Age theorist José Argüelles, identified the middle of August 1987 as a window of harmonic convergence. The specifics of exactly what that meant for humanity was vague, as mystical, pseudo-colonial cosmic events tend to be, but here's the gist: the planets in our solar system were forming triangle patterns that would help facilitate the creation of a "field of trust," enabling us to avoid annihilation, or contact extraterrestrial beings, or resurrect the Maya in the form of spectral feathered snakes. The predictions were hazy, but Argüelles claimed that something undeniably positive would happen if 144,000 people gathered in powerful places all around the world and meditated simultaneously. And people listened.

"There were even some predictions that the world would end on August 16," Johnny Carson said on his talk show. "And of course, it didn't—until tonight."

The studio audience laughed. I can't tell, watching boot-legged videos of the broadcast on YouTube, how much relief is speckled in with the outbursts of amusement, but there must have been some.

"Well, we think we know what went wrong," Carson explained, laying on the irony. "We counted all the people humming … we had a statistician run this down. We found out there were only 143,500 people humming. They were 500 people short."

Thankfully for the human race, the *Tonight Show* audience was 500 strong. For the sake of comedy, Carson got the masses to chant the om mantra. Between each soothing hum, he delivered a one-liner description of a miracle happening somewhere around the world, and while the whole thing was a comedy routine, he did, technically, satisfy the conditions of the harmonic convergence.

The world didn't end as our planet danced through Argüelles's window of cosmic change, but global peace wasn't exactly achieved either. Three weeks after the world's largest organized meditation event was bolstered by a live studio audience, I was born, and to me the world has never stopped ending.

"I wasn't sure having kids was responsible," my mom says, sipping from her beer. I had finally arrived at my parents' place, and we took to the water. Now we are sitting at the stern of a boat tied to the municipal docks of a town near their home while my dad pays for the slip. The sun is huge and yellow and soft behind the scorched atmosphere. Smoke from the wildfires on North America's West Coast reached us, activating my asthma, a chronic condition that I now sometimes worry is a symptom of the deadly virus ravaging our population. "I just thought it would be cruel. Or that we'd all die before the year 2000."

Mom has told me this before. She wasn't caught up in the harmonic convergence though. Her ideas of mass doom are firmly on the rational side of Armageddon. Nuclear war, pollution—fears I have shared as we weathered a procession of doomsdays together. I remember on the eve of the millennium debating if I should call my crush and confess my love before the Y2K bug deleted us. I remember January 2007, my ears still ringing from the gunshot that crumpled my dad, sobering up on a long walk home from my university pub and feeling like the frozen space between Downsview Station and Yonge Street was some lunar wasteland I was doomed to roam, a marauder in a personal post-apocalypse, having peaked with saving a parent's life at age nineteen. I remember in the winter of 2012, trying and failing to successfully pitch an ironic Mayan calendar apocalypse explainer to alt-weeklies. I remember the threat of atomic annihilation in January 2020, after the assassination of Qasem Soleimani via drone strike. And I remember the last day before the COVID lockdowns came to Halifax. I received an SOS email from my dad, who was trapped with my mom on a cruise ship in the Pacific. Trying to arrange a rescue flight home from Fiji, I wondered, *Is this going to be my last pre-apocalyptic memory?*

"How does it all make you feel?" Mom asks. "I wonder what you think about the future. Given all this."

"I guess I had to stop worrying about it and just trust that we'll adapt," I say. "A lot of what we're experiencing in terms of climate change are the consequences of actions made before I was born. It's hard to make a five-year plan in these conditions."

She thinks for a second and nods. "We all thought the world was dying. But maybe it's already dead. Maybe it's just taking a long time to end."

"I DON'T AGREE WITH THAT." My partner, Emma, sits in the passenger seat now, pinching and tapping the map on her phone screen. We're stuck in standstill traffic outside Quebec City, on our way home to Nova Scotia. While I was brooding with my mother, Emma was visiting with her own parents. "I don't think the planet is going to die with us."

Surrounded by other people in their vehicles, I'm acutely aware of the carbon dioxide we're all spewing into the atmosphere. I'm filled with a neoliberal guilt. Maybe we should have biked.

"Extinction isn't the death of the planet. That's human exceptionalism."

The car in front of me swerves into the emergency vehicle lane to catch a glimpse of what's causing this jam. It's the third time they've tried to scope out the situation. Whatever slowed us down must be far away.

"You're right," I say. "We have trouble in general, as humans, separating ourselves from the planet. All the climate scientists use Venus as an example of what's going to happen to us with a runaway greenhouse effect. But Venus is still around. It's still a beautiful, functioning planet. We just can't live there. We conflate the Earth's destiny with our own, but it doesn't depend on us."

"Exactly," says Emma. In the second wave of the pandemic, we streamed the BBC Earth series *The Planets*. Professor Brian Cox taught us about Venus's ultra-thick atmosphere, and how Mars doesn't have one because the sun licked it off. And he taught us that in five billion years, when the sun expands to a red giant, it might heat up the Saturnian moon Titan to the point where it could possibly support life just like Earth's. Just like us, but all over again. Or maybe not. Either way, it will be impossible for us to care.

The real death of the world will look like something out of a Junji Ito manga. Not many authors are comfortable ending their stories with the nullification of humanity, but Ito does it all the time. Whether we're twisted into oblivion by the spiral curse in *Uzumaki*, or strung up by sentient blimps that look like our faces in "The Hanging Balloons," our collective odds of surviving a Junji Ito story are slim. And then there's *Remina*, a cosmic horror graphic novel that sees Earth devoured by a planet-sized abomination, leaving readers with the final image of an abyss where we would otherwise see our pale-blue dot.

That pale-blue dot is still here, though, and I'm on it, merging across three lanes of bumper-to-bumper auto congestion trying to get to my exit. Traffic is proof that we continue to survive.

"I guess there wasn't an accident," says Emma, checking her phone. "The slowdown icon just looked like a collision icon."

Turns out we did this to ourselves.

HAUNTED VIDEOTAPE

THE TAPE ISN'T THE memory itself. It's plastic. Black with clear windows that let you peek in at the spooled-up ribbon. That's where the curse is. Light was captured, encoded, and magnetically sealed, waiting to be released through a near-forgotten ritual with obsolete technology. Buried in the deep shale of my family history, the curse slept benign, stacked and stored in the haunted chamber of the basement furnace room in my childhood home—a dark tomb filled with Tupperware bins of *Beast Wars* and Ninja Turtles and Batman action figures, participation ribbons for track and field, karate and hockey trophies, Grandad's skates, piles of school notebooks and graded tests and report cards we couldn't bring ourselves to throw away, and vintage Hot Wheels tracks we inherited and were tacitly expected to pass on to a coming generation.

Nick was excavating home videos. His plan was to digitize old recordings and store them on a hard drive that he'd give to our parents as a Christmas present. In his search, he uncovered a bounty. Videotapes labelled with masking tape. Videotapes labelled with official RCA stickers. Videotapes filled with birthday cakes, the forgotten voices of grandparents, and other tokens of our decades-old lives. Videotapes used for Saturday morning cartoon archiving. And one videotape that had been altered, unbeknownst to us, through the psychic shockwaves of trauma.

Nick crammed the tapes into his beige knapsack, threw in some tall cans of Pilsner, and shouldered them to the fourth-floor Toronto walk-up Emma and I called home. The building was nearly a century old and had recently survived a five-alarm blaze. Most of the units were still off-limits, their doors covered with orange and blue tarps. You could still smell the hint of smoke and blistered wood varnish. I think that's why the property managers offered us a free LCD flatscreen TV if we signed a year-long lease. That 720p Toshiba, connected to an old VCR by an umbilical cord of mixed-and-matched adapters, sat across from Nick as he pulled the tapes from his bag, then cracked his first beer of the night.

Emma and I sat on our white IKEA sofa, and the three of us watched the tapes one by one. Birthdays, Christmases, nursery rhymes, ABCs. The footage was all recorded on a big over-the-shoulder bazooka of a camera that Mom borrowed from work. We watched, we cringed, we laughed.

And then something different. A boy, me at four years, dying on the floor. Writhing and screaming, then rolling onto my belly and pushing myself up off the sand-coloured carpet to my feet.

"Bang!" The child me screams, jumps, hits the floor, and death wiggles.

"What are you doing?" My mom's voice comes from behind the camera as the little me works his way back to his feet, ready to die again.

"I'm playing shoot-explode," he says. "I get shot and I explode. Then I get back up and get shot again. Bang!"

The cycle repeats on screen. Shoot. Explode. Shoot. Explode.

My skin prickled with sweat, my solar plexus ignited with a deep burning. My breath shortened. I sucked my teeth.

"Oh no," I joked, "it's a premonition. Warn Dad!"

The scene passed, but the engine of my PTSD had already turned over. We continued watching the tapes, drinking, laughing, resurrecting childhood jokes, but half my mind was fixated on the game of shoot-explode. It was as if, by looking at this captured vision of my childhood, I had seen the face of my dad's shooter, heard the firework pop of the blue gun, felt the warmth of blood and the ache of my lower back under the weight of my father, who was losing consciousness in my arms, slipping away, getting heavier with every desperate step I took. All these sensations overtook me despite originating a full fifteen years after that home video was taken.

When the night was over and the tapes were tucked back in Nick's bag, I hugged him goodbye. Later, in bed, I fixated on my memories of Costa Rica, as I often do after a stressful day. Added to that familiar habit was a new scene from further back, a non-traumatic image now associated with the shooting. My trauma had somehow infected my forgotten past.

WHEN STORIES ARE RETOLD, they produce images and symbols that become independent of the actual text. It's a powerful effect and it's responsible for some of our culture's most enduring icons. My favourite example is the haunted videotape, a horror trope born from a series of adaptations and remakes. Introduced by Japanese novelist Koji Suzuki in his seminal novel *Ring*, the haunted videotape is now legendary, its mythology built up through four subsequent novels, a short story collection, a Japanese film adaptation and its sequel, a Korean film adaptation, and an American film remake of the Japanese adaptation, which itself has three sequels as of this writing. Each adaptation and remake is dramatically different from the version that came before it and spawns its own sequels that are unique from one another, but they all come from the same powerful point of origin: Suzuki's novel, the eye of the cultural hurricane.

In *Ring*, the haunted videotape is cursed by the vengeful telepathic energy emitted by Sadako, a dead psychic intersex woman who was sexually assaulted and thrown into a well. Her mental scream imprints an abstract series of images onto a videotape set to record a ball game, and anyone who watches those images is doomed to die of heart failure seven days later. That is, unless they allow its essence to reproduce, either through copying the video and screening it, writing down a description of the film and having someone read it, or through much more horrific biological means—in the book's sequels, humans with wombs infected by the viral media give birth to genetic copies of Sadako after an accelerated gestation period. In *Ring*, Sadako's trauma spreads to a journalist named Asakawa and his loathsome friend

Ryuji, whose quest to understand the mystery of the tape inadvertently unleashes the memetic contagion on the rest of the world, eventually resulting in a haunted videotape/ scary baby apocalypse.

The Japanese film adaptation makes significant changes to simplify the concept and enhance the theatricality of the original story. Directed by Hideo Nakata, the first movie version of *Ring* casts Asakawa as a woman, with a much more likeable Ryuji as her ex-husband, and ignores Sadako's intersexuality. Most notably, it introduces the most iconic image related to the haunted videotape: a drowned girl with long black hair climbing out of a well on TV, then crawling through the screen into our world to annihilate Ryuji. This image is brought forward into Gore Verbinski's *The Ring*, and is used in the sequels of both the Japanese and American franchises.

The films introduce a number of other symbols and concepts to the larger idea of the haunted tape. A phone call from a raspy stranger announcing you have seven days to live; physical manifestations of strange images from a psychic film; the American version of Sadako, Samara, a much more vengeful girl who was not sexually assaulted. These additions to the trope are undoubtedly more popular than the relatively minimalist version of the cursed cassette depicted in the original novel by virtue of how non-Japanese audiences were introduced to the concept. By the time we had access to Suzuki's *Ring*, the legend of the haunted videotape had already mutated.

Despite *Ring* having been originally published in 1991 (an astounding detail considering it originated the concept of a

viral video fourteen years before the launch of YouTube), the
first North American edition of the book didn't hit shelves
until after the films were already iconic for English-speaking
audiences. That means Anglo readers of the novel come to it
with preconceived notions of haunted videotape imagery. All
the extra supernatural stuff, including the set piece of Sadako
crawling out of TV-land into Ryuji's apartment, already lives
in the mind of the reader, but it is non-existent on the
page. The experience of reading the book is uncanny, as
Suzuki presents the words that inspired the cultural images
you expect, but that he never imagined himself. The past is
ensnared by the gravity of the future and cannot be experienced free of its inevitable context. This is the curse of linear
time, and it's how everything in the human world works,
from horror novels to home movies to history.

THE PHENOMENON WE CALL progress is a catastrophe.
That's what Walter Benjamin thought, and as far as I'm
concerned no one has ever been more right about anything.
In the ninth section of Benjamin's "Theses on the Philosophy
of History," the thinker fixates on the Paul Klee painting
Angelus Novus. If you google the painting, the first results
you see are bootlegged merchandise from custom swag
services like Redbubble and Society6, plastering Klee's work
on posters, phone cases, coasters, and custom sling chairs.
Which is fitting junk to bear Klee's abstract portrait of a
beast with an avian body, the head of a lion, and a mane
that looks like a tangle of unravelling scrolls. Its wings are
held up as if in worship or to protect its oversize face, and its

eyes are off-centre, giving the impression the angel is looking at something outside of its canvas. This detail must be why Benjamin describes it the way he does, proposing that it's beholding a storm blowing in from paradise.

"This is how one pictures the angel of history," writes Benjamin. "His face is turned toward the past. Where we perceive a chain of events, he sees one single catastrophe which keeps piling wreckage and hurls it in front of his feet." Benjamin's angel of history is caught up by an irresistible wind, making it helpless as the debris of time continues to pile up. "This storm is what we call progress," he concludes.

Taken together, Benjamin's eighteen meditations on history add up to a glorious takedown of capitalist and imperialist ideology, but the angel itself also illustrates a tragic aspect of our own relationship to personal memory. We are each our own *Angelus Novus*, caught in the wind and witnessing the gathering rubble of our own individual histories. We can't know what we are going to experience next, and whatever blows in from behind us will pile up on the ruins of our own pasts, obscuring our previous memories. The storm rages on, changing everything that came before it.

One only needs to consider Benjamin's own circumstances to see this effect in action. He wrote about the *Angelus Novus* while evading capture by the Nazis. On his way to Lisbon, where he expected to escape on a flight to the United States, France cancelled all travel visas, and Benjamin and his refugee party, having crossed into Catalonia, were prevented further passage by Spanish police. He killed himself by taking an overdose of morphine. The next day, his party was allowed onward to Lisbon after all, and his theses were passed on to philosopher Theodor W. Adorno, who helped get them published two years later, in memoriam.

The theses were completed before his death, but are obscured by the context of his demise. No one read Benjamin's final work when he was alive. This isn't necessarily a bad thing for the writing's core message—Benjamin's death acts as an exclamation point for the cruelty of history and the brutal stupidity of what we call progress—but it's an amoral effect. This is just how time, memory, and culture work. The purity of a moment, a thought, a memory, is immediately degraded by the next piece of temporal detritus blown in from paradise.

I USED TO BELIEVE that my memories were like dioramas, and that each time I contemplated them, I was accessing the original object. The intensity of my traumatic memories surrounding Dad's shooting are still incredibly detailed and invasive, and when they assault me, sending me into all sorts of physical and mental anguish, my instinct is that I am being tormented by one single memory: a piece of historical ruin that pushes itself to the front of the heap so it's always in view. But that's not what's happening.

Every time I remember December 27, 2006, I am occupying time and space. I am making history by virtue of my continued existence, and through my remembrance I am making rubble in the form of my previous trauma, which looms large under all its replicas. I am making piles of my own haunted videotapes, rerecording the same thoughts on different plastic tapes, each with its own context and flavour and atmosphere, slightly distorting certain bits, amplifying others, and contributing to the ruinous archive of my life. Replication, mutation, infection.

Sadako's trauma, first experienced by her, then imprinted on a tape and replicated memetically and biologically, spreads across the world until all that remains is her and the terrible things she remembers. A world overtaken by a single fixation on an unspeakable event. It's a metaphor for the insidious nature of trauma and the cancerous effect of replication. Monsters are born, hope is extinguished, and the present merges with the past until all that remains is traumatic homogeny. Annihilation through stasis. No more overwriting tapes, no more replicating memories—the storm has stopped blowing in from paradise and all that remains is a wasteland of uncannily symmetrical ruins.

It's probably important now to tell you that Sadako's world, and therefore the world of *Ring*, takes place in a simulation. In Koji Suzuki's third novel, *Loop*, the world has been overtaken by Sadako's memetic curse. We know this because it's revealed that the world of the first two books was a virtual construction contained in an underground super-computer, and that it crashed once all life had been killed or shaped into a physical manifestation of her trauma. The book sees a gifted young scientist named Kauru seek out the servers of the simulation so that he can try to understand how to cure a pandemic of viral cancer in the real world. The experience of reading *Loop* is incredible, as it completely changes the books that came before it without materially affecting them whatsoever. It simply infects the reader with new information that permanently transforms the writing's prior context. You read it, you can't unread it.

The experience of rereading *Ring* after reading *Loop* becomes one of reader revision. The supernatural elements of the book take on a digital aura, recontextualized as strange phenomena within a computer rather than paranormal happenings occurring in a haunted world made of water and rock. It doesn't dampen the experience, but it does dominate it, just as the major icons of the film adaptations have obscured the text's original effect. This one horror novel, by virtue of its effectiveness to produce sequels and adaptations, has grown into an immense monster outside its own pages. Our culture obsessed over the haunted videotape, replicated it, retold it, continued living with it, and in doing so created something greater than the sum of its parts, and that is, at the same time, inseparable from them.

Just as the simulation server in *Loop* contains the collapsed history of the preceding novels, our own lives compress under our personal angelic storms of history. New information, rediscovered memories, world events, and the act of remembering itself all contribute to the archive of our lives. Zoom out, take an angel-eye view, and you will see the patterns. All the cloned wreckage threading through your personal history, memories of memories strangling your narrative with oil-black ribbon, builds a mosaic of post-trauma. Guns, family members, boats, water, loud noises, good weather, holiday decorations, the ocean, strangers, and the performance of everything being fine, all coalescing into an emergent diagnosis: infection with bad memories.

There is an instinct I have when writing about this, fixated on my growing collection of wreckage and adding to it with every word that I type, to try and find a cure for the memetic virus in this video library, the haunted Blockbuster of my mind. Maybe there's a way out. A reset button. An exorcism ritual to appease the angry psychic ghost in my ruins. Maybe the footage will show me a well, underneath a resort, that I can spelunk into and repatriate the proverbial remains of my tormentor, finally laying the angry spirits to rest. Like Asakawa in *Ring*, I just need to find it and extract it and hope with all my heart I'm not giving life to something much more terrible than the event that started this syndrome. A monster outside of the tapes.

THE TRICK TO POISONING A SONG

PLAY THE RIGHT SONG and memory becomes a music video. Turn up the volume and let recollection tumble into a perfect montage of life's iconic moments. The teenage cliché of experiencing your first drug trip abbreviates to fit neatly within the two-and-a-half-minute crescendo of Jefferson Airplane's "White Rabbit." Every depressive episode of your life rains on Radiohead's "How to Disappear Completely." Suddenly your pathos feels poetic. Listen to The Kills and remember yourself at your leather-jacket coolest. Turn on Lorde and wrap profound memories in your high school uniform. It's cinematic. It's exciting. But it's a one-way relationship between life's important moments and the perfect accompanying playlist. Music can underscore and accent, it can juxtapose and inject irony, but it can't replace a sour mood or cleanse a dire vibe in the present moment. On the other hand, life can poison a song, and that's why it's dangerous to live with the stereo turned up loud.

In December 2006, my dad and brother were vinegar and baking soda. Their volatility, as I understand, was the result of Dad's bipolar, Nick's loneliness as a seventeen-year-old, and a lifelong rapport based on joke antagonism—the kind of teasing that's jovial in the good times but turns caustic with the mood. Everything one of them said made the other fizzle.

As an early Christmas present to himself, Dad purchased Cat Stevens's two-disc best-of album with a black-and-white close-up photo of the folk legend on the cover. The night before our flight to Fort Lauderdale where we would embark on our doom cruise, the CD spun in the family computer tower next to the kitchen table and Nick announced his departure.

"I'm going out." He already had his coat on. "I'll be back to throw my stuff in the car. Gonna sleep on the plane."

Stevens sang about freedom through the PC's speakers. The family plan was for us to pile into the car at 3:00 a.m. so we could make the drive to Toronto in time to push ourselves through post-9/11 airport security and make our early morning flight. Not the kind of thing you want to sleepwalk through, but Nick needed out of the house for one last party with his friends before being trapped on a boat with his family. Seventeen-year-olds can be so dramatic.

"If you're not back, we're leaving without you," Dad joked in the tone he reserved for my brother, coded with humour and frustration, like a line of classical theatre. I've always seen my brother and father as elevated personas, sharing a mythril-forged strength of will and righteousness. Nick is Pan, and Dad is something darker. Hades maybe, or Poseidon, or Zeus.

Their verbal sparring has always seemed electric, a display of might clashing in sparks of barbed wit and irony.

"I don't care." Nick grinned back. He put on his boots and a giant knit coat that made him look like a gnome. The door's weather-stripping made a smooching sound as he disappeared into the night.

Mom and Dad readied for bed and I packed my bag, watching the new holiday episode of *The Office* on my laptop, mulling over the family tension. Was I seeing the token reckless idea of a seventeen-year-old on holiday or was it the culmination of something deeper—in the past twelve months Nick lost an infant cousin and survived a brutal car crash. T-boned while making a left turn, he emerged from the driver's seat of the wreckage as the only conscious occupant. His three friends were still out cold when the first responders arrived. He walked home after that, taking a forest path shortcut to our house. I couldn't tell then, because we didn't talk much, but Nick felt like he was drowning at home.

Midnight came and the front door broke the silence. Nick was home early and my worry of further drama dissipated. With more than two hours before we were scheduled to roll out of the driveway, we were in good shape. No more snipping and sarcasm, no leaving Nick behind like some post-Culkin *Home Alone* sequel. But then I heard whispering, and the shuffling of stockinged feet outside my door confirmed there were visitors all slipping their way into Nick's room, which adjoined mine. His wooden bedroom door slammed shut, slapping the residual sleep off my face. The party guests revealed themselves by yelling and laughing and possibly playing music; I couldn't tell sounds apart in the growing cacophony.

Laughter, shouting, and a consistent thump-thump-thumping. Lying in the red glow of the digital alarm clock counting away the remaining minutes of possible sleep before our trip, I imagined Nick's room. Within its muraled walls that depicted many-eyed creatures, colourful neon portals, and a giant black-and-white peace sign, I pictured a bacchanal. Smoke from my brother's hookah clouding the toothy smiles of his friends, their lolling tongues, and wild, glassy eyes. One of them, judging by the persistent banging rhythm I could feel in my spine, was determined to bash a hole through the floor by stamping his foot.

Dad shouted from bed, his voice muted by Nick's vortex of yuletide revelry. Then he stood outside Nick's door. Radiating anger. First an appeal to reason unanswered. Then his hands, slamming against the door, rattling the hinges. The abomination of sound grew. Noise and joy and rage.

Dad flung open the door. Heat, energy, light, sound—an explosive reaction punctuated by the *boing* of the wire spring doorstop. But instead of a megaton blast, a corrosive silence underpinned a short, calm lecture. I couldn't make out the words, but Dad's voice was calm and controlled, and when he was done I heard feet shuffle out of Nick's room just as quietly as they'd entered. The weather stripping kissed the cold night air, ejecting the intruders through the family airlock.

The house was a crypt until the clock alarms woke us up. I dressed quickly and tossed myself into the back seat of my mom's red Honda Civic. Dad was already there, sitting in the driver's seat. The Cat Stevens jewel case lay on the centre console, black and white, his bearded face serene and wise. He preached through the speakers about singing out, about being free. About there being a million ways to be.

Mom wrangled Nick, who sat next to me without a word. The four of us rode to the airport, barely speaking and with zero acknowledgement of what had happened only a few hours ago. It seemed like an event that took place in another realm, one falling further away as Dad merged onto the highway. When Cat finished his folk manifesto, Dad thumbed the skip-track button on the black steering wheel. The lyrics in the next song begged us to relax, to take it easy. To understand that the turbulence of age is no one's fault. The song ended, Dad pushed the button, getting Cat to sing "Where Do the Children Play?" After that, it was back to the freedom song. We were stuck in a sonic loop.

The same three songs underscored the entire drive. The intention, I'm sure, was to diffuse the negativity and curate a calm atmosphere before the stress of airport security. To expedite the emotions we felt into the neat arc of a few folk songs. "If You Want to Sing Out, Sing Out," "Father and Son," "Where Do the Children Play?"—these were the best tunes on the best-of record. Wholly positive, focused on reconciliation and understanding. But that's not how music reacts with memory. Yusuf Islam cannot wash guilt, shame, and anger from the montage of a father-son conflict. But as it turns out, those emotions can blight his songs.

When I think about the events of the subsequent days, and the violence and the blood and the screaming and the psychosis, my recollections start with Cat's crooning and the clash of my family's strongest personalities. It plays in a perfect music video every time I hear those songs. An entire winter's night compressed into a few folksy minutes of platitudes and posivibes. Pure irony brewed in the reactive core of a car stereo. Cat Stevens is the sound of my family falling apart before a gunshot brought us back together.

MY OWN PERSONAL OVERLOOK

IN MY RESTLESS DREAMS, I see the ship. White like the tusk of a gargantuan beast, a sun-bleached blemish in the water. Sometimes I see it in the distance as a storm rolls in, the horizon turned into a strip of spoiled cream under dark purple clouds. I swim to catch up with the boat and board it before everything gets much worse. Screaming grows into a wall behind me, and I sense flailing bodies—too close, too squeezed, too submerged—thrashing and going limp. I add my voice to the cacophony. My own desperate cries. *Don't leave without me.*

Other times I'm on the ship already but I don't know it. At least not at first. I'm back in high school and forgot to go to religion class all semester, or I'm returning to my old job at the mall chocolate store, or I'm moving out of my old midtown Toronto apartment, manoeuvring pieces of furniture down the fire escape. I run through the halls of my school, trying to find my empty desk; I leave the store dragging a dolly to the cold room so I can restock the shelves with sweets; I look out the back door to see how much room is left in Dad's pickup truck for packed-up boxes of books, and suddenly I get it. I know where I am. The people around me are lotioned and swimsuited and preoccupied with drink and music and sun. The halls are dark and carpeted, lit by art deco wall sconces. Glass elevator tubes line grand atriums, like rib bones in the chest of a Fabergé whale. A grand piano, casino noises, and pools, pools, pools. My anxiety dream task is more complicated now. I still need to get to class, restock the store, move out of my apartment, but everyone is on vacation. I am on vacation. And when you are on vacation the rules are different.

VACATION DESTINATIONS ARE NOT great for productivity. Just ask Jack Torrance. The primary character of Stanley Kubrick's *The Shining*—a very liberal Stephen King adaptation—just wanted to get some writing done in the five months of solitude he signed up for when he took the job as winter caretaker for the Overlook Hotel. Built in 1907, the Overlook is a secluded mountain resort with a dark history. Built on stolen land, the cursed hotel was also the site of a gruesome familicide. Jack's most notable predecessor caught a spate of cabin fever, murdered his wife and twin daughters with an axe, then blew his brains out with a shotgun. The scars of the Overlook's history are hidden from the surface, but as the building's seasonally employed cook explains to Jack's psychic child, Danny, the place has a shine to it.

Jack, aware of the Overlook's history, thinks he has what

it takes to resist the madness. When his new employer, Mr. Ullman, warns him about the toxic solitude that comes with the new appointment, Jack puts a positive spin on it. "Turns out, I'm outlining a new writing project," he says. "Five months of solitude is just what I need."

Jack's working vacation is the end of him. The restless spirits in the hotel convince him to attack his wife and child with an axe, and he loses himself in the Overlook's hedge maze, freezing to death overnight. While it's easy to blame the ghosts for Jack's final rampage, a closer reading of Kubrick's film reveals it was a vacation that killed the recovering alcoholic.

The spectre of work hangs over Jack throughout his tenure at the Overlook, despite his view of the job as a writer's retreat and its status as a getaway destination. He stays up late at the typewriter, going berserk when he's interrupted. He uses work as an excuse to further isolate himself, worrying that he should finish some writing before joining his family on a late autumn walk through the hedge maze. He flaunts his contract to care for the hotel over his wife, Wendy, when she becomes concerned about his behaviour. And of course, when Wendy finally has her chance to read Jack's unfinished manuscript, we see the killer's burnout manifest: "All work and no play makes Jack a dull boy," written over and over again, thousands of times, formatted as if it were a coherent document, with indents, margins, even a page of triangle-themed concrete poetry. Chaos warped into the shape of order.

Jack's manifesto is vacation's perfect metaphor. Don't be fooled by its grotesque mimicry: a dream holiday is the swollen chaos we use to define the order of our working lives by contrast. Work is repetitive, toilsome, and done in service of an eventual reprieve. The break in the pattern is what we strive for, to finally relax, read a book, write a novel, spend time with the family. Broken patterns are also, not coincidentally, the core mechanic of horror. A horror story-teller establishes a pattern, which leads the viewer to a state of assurance. The pattern is broken, shattering expectations, and the result is an unnerving shock and the realization that patterns are unreliable, nothing is safe, chaos reigns.

The Shining is a special example of this horror effect in action, since the patterns it establishes are false from the outset. The carpet Danny plays on with his toy trucks changes underneath him, for instance. And each new scene in which Jack is writing shows him using a different typewriter. These details are nearly impossible to notice if you aren't looking for them, but once you see these subtle changes in the environment, the themes of the film click into place. You thought you were safe in the order of recognizable patterns—cause and effect, expectation and delivery, work and vacation—but the motifs were never properly established in the first place. Any time we point to something familiar, grasping for hard reality like Jack gesturing toward his work, we discover something alien instead. In the absence of the recognizable, we are left in a state of mental freefall.

The final shot of Kubrick's film further confounds our ability to ground *The Shining* in any sort of knowable reality. A photo shows Jack attending the Overlook's 1921 July Fourth gala as a staff member—something that would be impossible given his age and what we know of his life and work history. Taken literally, the picture further shatters whatever supposed order was left in the film, one final impossibility to further unnerve viewers. But allegorically, it widens the borders of the terrible labyrinth that is the Overlook Hotel.

The symbol of the labyrinth is not subtle in *The Shining*. Sure, there are eerily minuscule nods to it in the way Kubrick shoots the hotel, making its layout seem impossibly shaped, but the final confrontation between Jack and Danny literally takes place in a hedge maze. It's basic analysis: when you see a maze, you look for the Minotaur, and in *The Shining* it's obviously Jack, with his anger and his axe. That one-to-one comparison is often where this type of analysis stops. But in this case, it's worth remembering why the labyrinth was built.

There are people who hate Kubrick's adaptation of *The Shining*, including King himself. The primary criticism is that Jack has no arc. *He starts crazy*, they say. *It's not interesting if he doesn't change*. But that's the whole point. In Greek myth, King Minos commissioned the legendary artificer Daedalus to create the labyrinth in order to contain the Minotaur. The existence of the monster necessitated its prison, not the other way around. The Overlook, with all its nightmarish twists and turns and evil tapestries, depends on Jack Torrance. Jack has always been the Minotaur, and the Minotaur has always been in its maze. Vacation is a state of mind.

JAMES SUNDERLAND WILL NEVER escape Silent Hill. Drawn to the foggy resort town by a letter from his deceased wife, Mary, the protagonist of *Silent Hill 2* arrives of his own will in order to track down the source of the missive. As he finds his way deeper into the shifting nightmare world, populated by psychosexual monstrosities and a few other grieving and miserable characters, our protagonist comes to discover that years ago he euthanized Mary, who was terminally sick, by smothering her with a pillow.

The town of Silent Hill manifests itself as a psychological torture chamber, where visitors must constantly face physical representations of their own repression and guilt over past trauma. For James, the faceless nurses and shuffling collections of mannequin legs that attack him are Freudian embodiments of his conflicting love and regret, while the game's most iconic villain, Pyramid Head, is the manifestation of masculine rage turned inward. This bespoke prison quality of the town, strengthened by the game's shifting level design and dream-logic puzzles, makes it a true labyrinth.

Players have some agency over how James behaves, and that behaviour changes the outcome of the game. *Silent Hill 2* has multiple endings. The three main ones are generally considered to be truly alternate conclusions: James escapes Silent Hill alone, or with a woman who reminds him of Mary, or he dies by suicide by driving into a lake. But there are even more endings that can only be experienced after achieving the core three. The effect of playing through *Silent Hill 2* to collect the different endings is to tacitly admit that the story's conclusion doesn't matter as much as the journey. In the most infamous secret ending, James opens a door in the final area of the game to reveal an adorable Shiba Inu at a control panel, pushing levers and buttons, the canine puppet master of everything in the evil town. James collapses in tears, the dog comes to comfort him, and the credits roll.

When it comes to *Silent Hill 2* there is no satisfaction in a good ending or lasting pain in a bad ending. But there is truth in the dog ending. If, even after finding the pooch behind the curtain, you start another game (maybe you want to find the UFO ending, or the one where James resurrects Mary), you will start in the same place as you always do: the highway lookout over Silent Hill. If you navigate James away from the town, he will stop you. "This is the road I came in on," he says. "There's no point in turning back."

He's there, where he belongs, in this labyrinth made to contain him. Again and again, he pushes through the fog, seeking the source of his pain and finding familiarity.

THE SHIP IN MY dreams is infinite and recursive, but the real-life *Carnival Liberty* has twelve decks, each with their own names and special functions. Deck one, Riviera, and deck two, Main, are filled with cabins. Deck three, the Lobby, has the first floor of the dining room in the aft. It houses the galley for the crew and staff, and serves as the ground floor of a main common area that stretches all the way to the upper decks, providing an interior view to the occupants of the ship's glass elevators. Near the bow there's the orchestra level of the Grand Venetian Palace, a proscenium stage on which a troupe of recurring players will perform Vegas-esque song-and-dance numbers every night for the duration of your stay. Deck four, the Atlantic, doubles up the lobby, adding a second level to the restaurant and a mezzanine for the Grand Venetian, but instead of galley space, there's the Cabaret Lounge, one of many theme bars within the ship. Deck five is the Promenade, which houses three different bars in the aft, a café and arcade mid-deck, Club O2 (which sounds like an oxygen bar, but is actually a dance club for teens), a small casino, some shops, a view to the atrium, and the balcony level of the Grand Venetian. Decks six, seven, and eight, labelled Upper, Empress, and Verandah, are exclusively for cabins. Deck nine is the famed Lido Deck.

The Lido Deck hosts twenty-four-hour buffets, outdoor and indoor pools with waterslides, full bar service, and a stage for entertainment. This is where the indulgence of a cruise vacation lives. Lido is the last full deck, with open sun above it bathing the endless stretches of beach chairs in rays. The remaining three decks, Panorama (ten), Spa (eleven), and Sun/Sky (twelve), comprise the last of the cabins, a running track, and some fitness facilities, and they all look down on the Lido Deck, which has the feeling of the ground floor of a colosseum.

Lido is where, on the first day of the cruise, the entertainment director leads a bunch of semi-nude strangers in party games and icebreakers in an attempt to make everyone abandon shame. And it works, at least every time I've seen it. Hooting and whooping, the crowd gathers on the Lido and Promenade, encircling the cruise director in his shades, branded golf shirt, and wearable microphone. He solicits men of all shapes and sizes for the customary hairy chest competition. Without fail, among the participants is a plucky child, hairless save for his golden head. The cruise director walks the line of bodies, pointing, requesting they pose, and goading the audience to vote by applause: which of these bodies is most acceptable in spite of its unsightly hair? How welcome are these monsters here in this labyrinth of excess? The living applause-o-meter roars, with "awoogas" and "ow-ow-ows" peppered in by any friends and family members who haven't fainted in embarrassment. When it's time to cheer for the child, the adoration is too much. The hairless Theseus breaks the scale.

You won't see it on the ship's floor plan, and it seems like a given in the 2020s, but there is a preponderance of hand sanitizer stands placed throughout the ship at every threshold. In 2006, this was a precaution necessitated by the vessel's previous outing in which cruisers contracted norovirus. Twelve decks meant for pleasure turned into an anxious bathroom line by a common virus. Plan for relaxation all you want, but there are no guarantees on vacation. Itineraries, brochures, the confidence of the cruise director, a spreadsheet calendar of how much fun you intend to have—futile attempts to fence off and domesticate the monsters outside our fragile society. They're all in the *Liberty* with you. The penitentiary you constructed based on everything your life didn't have. A maze of twenty-four-hour gambling, drinking, and baking under an oppressive sun. Family tension. Echoes of epidemic. A blue gun with a bullet inside. Blood. Screaming. Concussion. All the pleasure and violence normally kept at bay by life's mundanity, squeezed into a place you go when you close your eyes.

When I was twenty-one, I tried to turn my *Liberty* dreams into a play. An auto-fictional account of my time on the ship, filtered through the expressionist interpretation of my recurring nightmares. Near the end of the two-act dramedy, the labyrinth metaphor is realized through a series of monologues on family trauma. It is clear, rereading my script that at the time I wrote it, two years after the inciting event, that I thought the gunman was the Minotaur. But it was me all along.

When I dream of that ship—and I am coming to suspect every dream of mine is set somewhere in there—I must accept that it is part of me. A place my mind constructed out of some need to connect the dots between my chaotic time on the *Liberty* to the toil of work, education, and life after survival. My own personal Overlook. The Silent Hill I return to nightly. Not to find an answer, but because it's the twisted fantasy resort I built to confine myself. Wish you were here.

HOW HIGH CAN YOU KICK?

"STAND UP," SAID THE Man in the Blue Gi. And we did.

Mom and I stood in the dimly lit office. The room's only window looked out onto the padded area where a young man counted loudly in Japanese, each number prompting his dozen students to punch the air in front of them. Blinds obscured the view, but we still heard the punctuated hissing of the students breathing in unison.

"Trudy," said the Man in the Blue Gi. "How high do you think you can kick?"

"Oh," she said, pursing her lips and shaking her head. "I don't know."

"Just guess. Or even better: kick as high as you can."

She swung her leg like a pendulum, her toe peaking just above her waist.

The Man in the Blue Gi held his hand out, palm down, about a foot higher than Mom's first attempt. "Now kick my hand."

"That's too high."

"You can do it. Just kick my hand."

She shook her head. She took a breath. She swung her leg. She touched the hand with her foot.

"Great job," he said, beaming but unsurprised. He turned to me and repeated the process. Sure enough, when I needed to, I could kick higher.

"Karate training is going to be about what you just did," he said. "Me and the other instructors, your fellow students, we will ask you to do things you think are beyond your limits. They aren't. Everyone here helps everyone else do what they used to think was impossible."

I was thirteen years old. The demonstration struck me as simple and effective. And it sunk in. Years later, when I wore my own blue gi and taught my own new students, I mimicked the kicking demo because it really did encapsulate the core of martial arts. An intangible quality, deeper than faith and community—one I can only really explain with the help of anime.

MY INTEREST IN MARTIAL arts began as a fantasy, and that fantasy is titled *Dragon Ball Z*. Based on Akira Toriyama's *Dragon Ball* manga, *DBZ* is a television anime that ran from 1989 through 1996, chronicling the adventures of the legendary warrior Goku, an alien who was sent to Earth as a child to destroy all civilization and make way for intergalactic land brokers. A bonk on the head erased his villainous mission from his mind, and a succession of martial arts masters turned the tables on fate, transforming him from an invading destroyer into our planet's great defender. Now, he balances saving the world from evil forces with his duties as a new father.

While Goku's alien heritage grants him a natural proclivity for fitness and combat, his special abilities are all earned through dedicated martial arts training. Goku does push-ups and stomach crunches, practises hand movements and stances, and he meditates. His perseverance through toil and his desire for self-improvement are all it takes for him to eventually punch through mountains, move faster than the eye can see, fly through the air, and focus his ki into weaponized energy projectiles that he shoots from his hands.

Goku is not the only character in *Dragon Ball Z* with these abilities, which can be learned by anyone who fully dedicates themselves to unlocking their inner potential through training, as long as they have the right teacher. Goku's human friends can fly and shoot energy beams, and so can his half-human children, Gohan and Goten. The result of this accessible superpower mythology is a rare type of fantasy that challenges the audience to try being great themselves. Goku and his friends aren't plucked from orphanhood to attend a school for wizards, nor are they made to struggle with a mutant x-factor that can be harnessed into a unique miracle ability. They simply see their personal limits and know they can surpass them. They want to kick even higher.

Enchanted by *Dragon Ball Z*'s fantasy of martial arts magic, I obsessed over arcane violence and found karate. Being strong or fast or big is not enough to make someone a good fighter. Intellect and spirit also enhance a martial artist's power. In *DBZ*, massive musclemen are regularly presented as cruel dullards, and even the most powerful brutes are brought to beg before the relatively tiny likes of our more powerful heroes. Power is a product of a healthy body and mind, one that can withstand the overwhelming arcane energy unlocked through special learned martial arts techniques.

The most iconic of these special moves is the legendary Kamehameha Wave, taught to Goku and his best friend Krillin by the island hermit Roshi, master of the Turtle School. The technique requires a martial artist to focus their vital energy into a ball, gather it between their hands near their hip, and hurl it forward, all while chanting, "ka ... me ... ha ... me ... ha!" The kamehameha can only be learned through tutelage and dedication, meaning anyone who can use it has participated in the community required for learning, and has exemplified the indomitable spirit required for self-improvement. The kamehameha is a teachable technique, and it trumps all others because the most powerful forms of arcane violence belong to the virtuous.

When I was thirteen, I knew the kamehameha wasn't real. But I wanted to find the closest equivalent. So I started training.

DRAGON BALL Z IS AN ascension narrative. It doesn't have arcs. It's all incline. A powerful threat wreaks havoc and threatens the existence of life in the galaxy; our heroes train to get stronger and master new special techniques, they confront and defeat the evildoer, and then train for the next threat, who is inevitably more powerful and dangerous.

Along the way, our heroes grow stronger as a community, welcoming former rivals to their side—the demon king Piccolo, the three-eyed monk Tien, and the proud alien prince Vegeta—and growing their families. Everyone within Goku's orbit joins him on an upward trajectory with no apparent end, always doing their best to get better.

When I was a white belt, it was the allure of arcane violence that motivated me. Before joining karate I wanted to take tai chi. Catholic school's mythology of saints who could perform elemental miracles caused me to fixate on learning how to do the pious magic ascribed to the likes of Saint Aidan of Lindsfarne or Joan of Arc. (Which of course sounds delusional, but consider that I was taught that holy magic existed by teachers and priests in the same classrooms where I learned about math, biology, and chemistry.) My friend Daniel, who taught himself Bruce Lee's Jeet Kune Do from a book, showed me his bootlegged copy of the 1993 action comedy *Tai Chi Master*, starring Jet Li and Michelle Yeoh. The film had the quality of the Catholic saint myths I was researching for my confirmation sacrament. Jet Li played the historical founder of tai chi, Junbao, who in the film's climax learns to harness the wind into a kamehameha-esque projectile.

Yes, I thought. *This man was real. This story is real. Just like the saints. I can become like them. I can learn magic.*

The tai chi school wouldn't allow a power-hungry thirteen-year-old to join their meditative practice, so Mom persuaded me to try karate. We enrolled in the trial program together, and the Man in the Blue Gi convinced her to train with me. Together we attended adult classes on weeknights and reviewed our katas and self-defence techniques at home. We did push-ups and stomach crunches, and learned the basic punches, kicks, and blocks, each of which had its own intricate set of movements.

When I was a yellow belt, I signed up for my first tournament. Dad dropped me off in the dojo parking lot where I met Senpai Drew, a young instructor who invited me to carpool with him and two other black belts in his red Toyota Supra he sometimes raced on weekends. I was too novice to fight, so I performed my kata, Pinan Nidan, in a high school gymnasium for a panel of judges. I came third last, or eighteenth place, whichever sounds less humiliating. The ribbon I picked up from the trophy table called me a "finalist." It was my first public defeat.

When I was an orange belt, I started sparring. Mom bought us each a set of dark-blue protective gear—soft helmets, light gloves, foot pads, mouthguards—and on Thursday nights we suited up and fought our classmates. As a teenager, it is rare to fight your own mother with uppercuts and roundhouse kicks. I know she hated the experience, but endured it as part of the practice. I remember she had a practical attitude toward the overwhelming aspects of our training.

"If I ever need to use it in real life," she said, "I can't expect some bad guy to stop and start over so I can get him in an arm lock."

Sparring tests your grit. Can you keep a cool head and apply complex arcane techniques in the heat of kumite? The adrenalin of fighting in a safe and controlled environment is often enough to turn an orange belt into a punching bag. Week after week, bruising our shins and sometimes bloodying our noses or lips, we accustomed ourselves to the slow-motion high of mock combat.

When I was a green belt, I became obsessed. I could look back and see how far I'd come, but I could also look forward and see where I was heading. The belt after green in my school was called green-stripe—it was a green belt bisected all the way through with a thin black line. I focused on its colours as I trained in front of the dojo mirrors, as if the belt were revealing my goal. Black belt excellence was what Shihan, our school's founding master, called it. When I was green-stripe, I was allowed to start weapons training.

When I was a purple belt, I needed a job, so I applied to be an instructor. And when I was a blue belt, the Man in the Blue Gi became my co-worker. Shihan was my boss. I made my first work friends, Christy and Becca—black belt sisters who went to the public high school downtown. And crucially, I was given a key to the dojo. That meant on Saturdays when Christy, Becca, and I were charged with running the full set of weekend classes, I could show up extra early to be alone in the sacred space.

Martial arts is about community. But it's also about your relationship with yourself. It's about understanding your whole being—body, mind, and spirit. While community can support, drive, push, and inspire you to new echelons of prowess, I found moments of solitary training essential for exploring the connections between who I was and who I wanted to be. The dojo's mirrors helped me to see my stances, strikes, kicks, and blocks. They showed me where the lines needed straightening, where my feet needed adjusting, where my shoulders needed squaring. They also showed me an image of myself—my own student. In those moments of quiet, I felt whole.

When I was a brown belt, I feared I was running out of time. As a teacher, I had intimate knowledge of our curriculum's pacing. I was sixteen, it was winter, and I needed to graduate to the final pre-black belt, brown-stripe, by the summer. If I missed that checkpoint, I would not qualify for the sixteen-week black belt grading program that culminated in November. The fall after that I intended to be in Toronto, attending university. This was my only chance. I needed to accelerate my ascension.

"Shihan," I said after tasking a class of green belts with a set of twenty-five push-ups, "I need to go faster."

He stood in the doorway between the dojo mats and the front office. Through the windows behind him, I could see dusk gathering in the parking lot. He looked at me with his piercing eye contact and infectious smile. "Let's do it."

DESPITE WHAT YOU MIGHT infer from *Dragon Ball Z*, there are limits to what the human body can do. But those limits can be surpassed by technology. For the martial artist who seeks unity of mind, body, and spirit through the pursuit of arcane violence, the technology of warfare presents an existential quandary: why learn to fight with your empty hands when it's so much easier to hold a gun?

In his memoir *Raw: My Journey into the Wu-Tang*, New York rapper U-God dedicates a chapter to the relationship between the arcane and technological sides of violence.

When he was growing up in the Staten Island projects in the 1970s, fighting with fists was more common than shootings. U-God describes the importance of the hybrid martial arts manual *The 52 Hand Blocks*, and he bemoans the decline of non-mortal combat on two grounds. First, that a street fight can breed respect between enemies and rarely results in deathly injury. Second, guns have nothing to do with your character. Anyone can use a gun, says U-God. A blindfolded two-year-old can use a gun.

Technology offers a shortcut to the ends of the arcane. An entire lifetime of training can produce a martial artist capable of physical feats that seem superhuman. I have seen masters jump so high and with such ease that it seems as though they're flying as they spin into a hook kick and smash a concrete block to dust with one touch of their heel. It looks like magic. But the value of such control and strength is challenged, if not outright nullified, by an assailant with a firearm.

It was Halloween when the Man in the Blue Gi taught me and Mom about guns. Martial arts schools are made up of families, so trick-or-treating takes precedence over training. Only one other student was there, a green belt named Valerie, making four of us if you included our teacher.

"Can anyone tell me"—he pulled a wooden prop pistol from the folds of his blue top—"what to do when a person threatens you with a gun?"

We each proposed the self-defence moves we knew that might disarm a gunman. Throws, wrist locks, takedowns that control the arm holding the weapon.

"Those are all good, but the real answer is: you run."

A gunfight is not a fight. It's a deadly race against a trigger finger.

"You can't dodge a bullet," said our sensei. "Especially at close range. But most people who would use a gun to mug you are not particularly great shots, so if you run and rapidly change direction, chances are you will save yourself. If you're cornered, give the mugger what he wants. Your wallet, your jewellery. None of it matters in comparison to your life. And if he intends to do you harm, and if you can't run, here is what you can do."

The gun defences were quick and brutal. The aim was to disarm and disable. Break bones, toss the gun far. Even using a prop, I remember feeling a knot in my diaphragm every time I passed in front of the barrel, each infraction representing a brush with hypothetical death. I'd never seen a real gun before, but the scenario we laid out was high enough stakes that I learned to hate them. The escalation of brutality called for wilder techniques. We were allowed to bite. We were encouraged to gouge. If we ended an encounter with the gun in our possession we were instructed to shoot the attacker or throw the gun as far as we could.

"If you threaten him back, you can't risk him calling your bluff."

In the face of technological violence, we are humiliated. The first time Goku is truly outmatched is in the Android Saga of *Dragon Ball Z*, when he and the other protectors of Earth are confronted by the perfect artificial lifeform: Cell. A biological machine created in a lab, Cell never trained a day in his abominable life. All of his power is stolen from the human victims he absorbs for energy. He is stronger. He is faster. And if he gathers his hijacked ki into a ball near his hip, he can throw it forward in a beam. Technology stole the kamehameha.

Cell embodies an existential threat to Goku and friends. Like a gun to the martial artist, he represents the futility of human perseverance in the face of technology. It's the automation. It's the convenience. It's the inhuman nature of a shortcut to perfection. That's why Earth's victory against Cell is a moral one, steeped in metaphor.

When Cell is initially on the ropes, he initiates a self-destruct function powerful enough to obliterate the planet. As a machine striving for perfection, annihilation of all life is a technical achievement of his purpose. Goku steals the exploding android away to another planet, which is promptly destroyed along with our hero. But that's not the end of Cell. The monster re-forms on Earth, even more powerful than before. Only this time, we don't have Goku to protect us.

Gohan, Goku's son, is the only warrior strong enough to even try to fight Cell. And he does poorly. The machine is unstoppable, and mortals have their limits. Gohan's broken arm dangles at his side, useless. His friends—the best mortal warriors in the universe—watch from nearby cliffs, paralyzed with the knowledge that they're powerless in the face of Cell's technological superiority. And it is here, staring down the smug face of death, that Gohan exemplifies the true virtue of the martial artist. A gun can't fire a bullet from an empty chamber. But faced with a similar limit, the martial artist pushes forward where technology grinds to a halt. With one good arm, Gohan gathers his ki near his hip, chants the syllables. Pushed well beyond all boundaries of expectation, he remembers the example of his father and he fires a final kamehameha.

HOW FAST CAN YOU RUN? In my memory the whole journey started accelerating as soon as Shihan removed my brown belt and replaced it with a brown-stripe.

"Well done, Petey," he said. My work colleagues had taken to calling me Sempai Petey in front of my kids' classes. A term of endearment and, partially, an acknowledgement that I was the only staff member without a black belt. It was June when I earned that last colour belt. My black belt trials would begin in August.

They called us the black belt candidates. Jennifer, Katja, and I were graduating to our first degree, Nate and Travis to their second degrees, and Julie was striving for her third degree. The first thing we had to do was run. Over the span of sixteen weeks we had to jog a five-kilometre course forty times, recording speed improvements on a spreadsheet in a communal binder as we progressed. That broke down to roughly three runs per week, with two extra heats to be fit in at our own discretion.

The test was simple and elegant: can you accept the martial artist's lifestyle of consistent challenge? The forty runs, if saved to the last conceivable moment, would be a trial of destruction rather than a gauntlet of preparation. Your speed would decline from one run to the next, your body would pound itself into the sidewalk, your test would be over before it started—the point of running, after all, was to ready us candidates for a gruelling two-day grading that was legendary in its difficulty. Running was the preliminary test, but it was also the training for the main event. For a hope at ascension, you had to start on week one. So that's what we did.

Stopwatch in hand, legs stretched, and shoes tied tight, I loaded a CD into my brother's anti-skip Panasonic discman—the Offspring's *Smash*, the Mars Volta's *Frances the Mute*, Linkin Park's *Meteora*, the *Kill Bill* soundtracks, or a mix burned on my family computer of anything with a persistent beat and the kind of vibe that could push a seventeen-year-old boy through walls of exhaustion. I hit *play* and started the timer simultaneously.

Shihan traced the course himself, a five-kilometre tangle of sidewalk. Starting across from the Tim Hortons near the dojo, I ran a straight path on level ground through suburban strip mall sprawl before hanging a left into a pocket subdivision of two-storey houses with old-growth trees shading their front lawns. The sidewalk track sagged into a crescent, which spat me out onto a busy road across from a brown brick shopping centre. From there I turned right and ran up a steep incline, where the sidewalk bordered small houses with verandas. At the top of the hill, I made another right, which brought me onto the straightaway back to the dojo, but when I hit the entrance to the pocket neighbourhood, I turned into it again, ran the crescent, back up the hill of front porches, and entered the true home stretch.

The season changed and the course made its mark on my body, which—aided by my continued work and in-class training—thinned down to its efficient basics. I began to see running as a modular test. I would hit a limit, my body would scream to stop, and I would invent a checkpoint. *This is how far I think I can run.* And once I was there, I would glance at the stopwatch, skip to a faster song, and pick another checkpoint. The process shifted my mindset. The leaves changed colours, the first dusting of snow appeared, and I stopped seeing each run as an individual unit. I was participating in a forever race against myself, and I measured my victories by my ability to ignore whatever limitations and doubts floated in front of me. I was running too fast to see them. I left them broken like rubble on the sidewalk. I was transforming. And eventually the confidence I developed would be the subject of my final test.

IF YOU COLLECT THE seven titular Dragon Balls, which are scattered all across the planet, the dragon Shenron will appear and grant you any wish you desire. A hallmark of the villains in *Dragon Ball Z* is that they wish for supreme power: eternal life, unsurpassable strength, a shortcut to the end. Our heroes don't want that. They use the wishing orbs to reverse the tragedies caused by the power-hungry. They turn death back into life and repair communities. They protect their family. They understand there is no value to unearned power.

I was sworn to secrecy about the actual events of my black belt grading. What I can say is that it was spread over two days. First, we were in the dojo. We were isolated from each other. We were pushed past our limits. At one point, during a delirious sparring match with my co-worker Skyler, I caught a roundhouse kick in my mouth. Blood spurted onto the mats, my nerves numb from exhaustion and adrenalin. Mom, who was invited to watch, was furious. I iced it, put a pocket of gauze in my lip, and continued. The next morning, the six of us candidates met at Shihan's ranch. The pale-blue sky was airbrushed with white clouds, and the November sun lit the scene at such an angle as to freeze the forests we ran through in a state of perpetual sunrise. This time we could fight as a team.

When he launched his final kamehameha at Cell, Gohan was acting alone—a broken teen releasing all of his violent energy in a bid for life. It wasn't enough. The evil android's own blast was threatening to consume the boy in annihilating light. Gohan's friends, insects compared to the powers at play, joined the fight. Launching attack after ineffective attack in a fireworks show of pure moral support, they demonstrated exactly what the martial artist strives for: perseverance in the face of the impossible.

As I ran, as I leaped, as I hit wall after wall of exhaustion, fully fledged black belt students, each with their own memories of gradings past, emerged from the fields and out of the trees. They ran beside us, they cheered us on. I found my strength again and again, dragging my body forward even when my limbs went limp. Each word of encouragement strengthened my resolve, boosted my spirit. I was flailing. I was ascending. I was Gohan obliterating himself to achieve something unimaginable.

The scent of smoke in the air signalled the end. My fellow candidates and I sat in a circle around a campfire deep in the woods. Shihan was there, and he met each of our eyes with quiet pride. The flames were welcoming, but they stung my skin too. After a certain amount of adrenalin and pain, the body is reluctant to receive even the primal comfort of a bonfire on a cold morning.

"What you did today was the beginning of something special," Shihan said. "Some day, you will need to surpass your limits. It might not be for a very long time. But you will remember this day, and you will remember what you did with one another, and you will find the strength you know you have. You will rise to the occasion."

THE BELT WAS HEAVIER than the coloured ones I was used to. Thicker. More durable. I worked at the dojo with it tied around my waist and it weighed on my hips, grounding me and strengthening my pride. Shihan gave me access to his vhs library of katas and weapons techniques, which is how I taught myself to use the three-pronged sai. I kept training. I kept teaching. But I knew my time was limited and I feared what that meant for my accomplishment. My black belt was probationary.

In order to disincentivize black belt tourism—in which bad faith students participate in karate, achieve the internationally recognized symbol of excellence, and move on to their next hobby—Shihan mandated a full year of probation. It was called shodan-ho. For twelve months, newly christened black belts had to maintain their regular training and volunteering, after which they would be granted a certificate and official first-degree black belt status.

With three months remaining on my trial period, I moved to Toronto for theatre school, suspending my probation and entering into a dojo-less limbo. Shihan burned me a DVD of videos in which he performed kata and self-defences. I trained on my own in my building's fitness centre. I maintained, but I didn't move forward. And when November came and I inevitably had to stay in Toronto for my exams and student perfcrmances, my window for official black belt status closed.

The next summer I returned to the dojo and was allowed to train in the black belt class without question. Mom was still attending classes, preparing for her own candidacy the next year. No one mentioned my lack of official status, and I hoped my show of dedication as a returning student would suffice.

In the fall I went back to Toronto, and that winter I would be tested again.

I STOOD ON THE wooden pier, overdressed. Blue jeans, black leather belt and a green hoodie over a T-shirt I got from the 2004 Canadian Open Martial Arts Challenge. The gunman stood between Dad and me, poking the barrel of his blue pistol at each of us. The ocean roared at our backs. The Man in the Blue Gi flashed in my mind. *Whatever you have isn't worth dying over.* But we were cornered and we left all our money on the ship.

Dad kicked at the man. Once. Twice. And then he fell. My eardrums screeched from the gunpowder pop. I ran to my father as the shooter fled.

"He bit me."

"You got shot?"

"He bit me."

"Did he shoot you?"

"Yes."

I helped Dad to his feet. Slung his arm over my shoulder, and we stumbled on our way to safety. I dropped him. Three times. My body screamed. I screamed. Dad's eyes fluttered shut and I was weak. My mind flickered through a million useless sounds and images, searching via free association for any ember of hidden motivation that could get me through to the other side. Scenes from TV shows, memories of previous vacations, Nick and Mom's itinerary, the map to the ship, the prayers I memorized in school. The tournament where I got my shirt, how Dad bought it for me after winning a gold medal for the first time in my life. There was no one left to fight, but I frantically grasped at memories of my training. The gun defences. The smell of sweat. The familiar burning of overworn muscles. I thought of a hand held out in midair, challenging me to kick higher.

I pushed myself from the ground and began to drag Dad toward the ship. Today, when I remember that moment of finding strength, a wire gets crossed and I swear I can smell smoke from a bonfire.

TIME SICKNESS

GREEN, HEAVY CREAM, BROWN like dry soil. I see these colours when I think of 1918, the date on the hardback copy of H.G. Wells's *The Invisible Man* that once belonged to my grandfather. The book itself is faded green, and holding it evokes a satisfying art-gallery calm. I have been told many times, usually after I've published something that has caught the attention of my family, that Grandad was an enthusiastic writer of letters who knew his way around the English language. The way Dad would always correct my brother's grammar and syntax felt like a legacy reflex, and the only time I've ever used an electric typewriter was the Christmas my parents gave one to Grandad. I am proud to be compared to him, my namesake—John William by birth, Bill to his friends, Pete during the war for old-timey reasons that are still unclear to me. We have a similar build and a similar smile. We both experienced violence as teenagers.

The Wells novel is a strange artifact. I saw Grandad

as a serious man who survived a war and enjoyed sports. The volumes that lay around his home were baseball-stats compendiums and photo books about various military seacraft with titles like *Dog Boats of World War II* and *Aboard the* HMCS *Haida*. I didn't expect he would like fiction, let alone science fiction. It's one of the many things I never asked him about. I loved him but I feared him, and when he died, my opportunity to understand the extent of our similarities was extinguished.

BLACK TYPE ON A white screen. Words and numbers and the names of colours. This is a test. Match them up, don't overthink it, the timeline is real and unchanging. Trust in what you see: the hue of September, the distance from 1987, the brilliance of the number three. Space-time synesthesia is a way of naturally perceiving time, in which the person in question sees colour and shapes when thinking about hours, days, weeks, months, and years. I always thought it was an insignificant phenomenon, first because I assumed this was how everyone saw time, and second because when I initially encountered other so-called space-time synesthetes our conversations were absurd and frustrating, since the aesthetics associated with a given unit of time are different for everyone. While Thursday is a stormy blue with hints of yellow for me, it might be a vibrant pink for someone else, and we're both right, and no one else in the world cares. But I am taking this test—part of a University of Michigan study on the phenomenon—because it matters to me.

The way I see time is, conceptually, not unlike Kurt

Vonnegut's description in his anti-war novel *Slaughterhouse-Five*. The four-dimensional aliens who abduct protagonist Billy Pilgrim illustrate time as a static phenomenon that can be observed from afar like a mountain range. At one point on the range, Billy Pilgrim is in a Dresden prison camp, at another he's being born, at yet another he's in an alien spaceship learning about the shape of time. At another point he's dead.

For me, time has always been more of a line than a mountain. It twists and turns with the passage of days and weeks, folding up and down with each night and day. When I think about periods of time—imagining the setting of a book or film, or remembering a time in my own life—the decades have prevailing colour schemes and I see the timeline against a backdrop of a secondary shade of white or black or light blue. If this makes no sense, I'm sorry. The reason I'm taking the test is twofold: I want to help academics put the time colours to some kind of practical use, and I want to confirm a suspicion. In the mid-2000s, my timeline changed. It used to be a grand tapestry woven from brilliant filaments of emotion and association and memory. Now it is a single red thread stretching through a starless void. Flavourless. Dull. Sick. And I wonder if engaging with my synesthesia actively will help me get it back to normal.

THE MID-1990S ARE GREEN laced with gold and blue. It was during that stretch of years that I held a misshapen piece of heavy glass. It used to be an ashtray, but no longer held any function except as a souvenir or paperweight. It was transparent and intact. I expected it to be jagged and sharp, but either time dulled the edges or rifle rounds interact with ashtrays in unexpected ways.

"Grandad," I asked, sitting on the couch in the television room of his bungalow, his tube TV flickering with satellite signal. He stood in the double-wide doorway, overtop of which he'd mounted two hockey sticks, signed by famous players and crossed like bones on a pirate flag. "What was it like when the sniper shot the ashtray out of your hand?"

He jutted out his jaw and stretched his lower lip across his teeth. Looked at me with a rare scowl. "Why would you want to know about something like that?"

The war seemed romantic to me. A time of heroes, like Grandad, and villains, like the sniper. I wanted to understand the emotional details so I could imagine myself in his wool navy jacket, immersed in sea fog and the scent of loose tobacco. I knew the basics, so I sought answers to impractical questions. What was it like to take a smoke break during World War II? Did he feel any kind of ominous dread? What did his buddies think? Did they catch the gunman, and if not, does he wonder what happened to his would-be assassin?

His reaction shut me up. At the time, I was incapable of understanding that something so far in the past could still hurt, but it was clear I crossed a threshold. I never asked him about the war again.

THE THIN RED WIRE stretches across infinite black. Like a laser through the abyss. This isn't how it's supposed to be.

I can't see time anymore. Not the way I used to. I am sitting in my therapist's home office. I tell him about the line. I tell him about my trouble. How this might sound crazy, but the 2000s weren't this colour before. Just a few years ago, time was rich with hints of gold on peppermint swirls of red and white. But now it's just this diminished piece of floss.

"Tell me more about this line," he says. And I describe the tangle it emerged from. The tapestry of my personal history ends in a messy knot, on December 27, 2006, at around eleven in the morning. A dense ball of memory cutting off circulation to whatever parts of me sense time, like an elastic band wrapped too tight around a fingertip. The tangle is massive, and it's growing, and I feel pulled toward its gravity.

"Describe that feeling," he says. "What do you feel when you see this tangle?"

I stammer and ramble as language fails me. I don't have the words, but I can compare it to other horrid sensations. It's the retracting cringe sensation you feel when reading the passage in *Slaughterhouse-Five* about the villain Paul Lazzaro and what he did to that poor dog—sticking a bunch of sharp shrapnel in a raw steak and feeding it to the mutt, then watching it writhe and vomit and die. In the future, when Ryan North and Albert Monteys adapt Vonnegut's story into a graphic novel, they will distill the scene into three panels. The colour they use for the dog's insides is the prevailing tone of the tangle. The full sensory experience of insides torn out.

I tell my therapist that when I think of the tangle, I get confused about when and where I am. But I don't tell him about the urge to scar myself, that I want to manifest the tangle on the outside to prove it exists. To prove my trauma happened. To make my sickness more than an abstract set of images tying me to the memory of a pier, a gun, and a stranger with angry eyes.

Once, I decided to dig into my chest with razor blades, but I cut my thumb when drunkenly trying to loosen an edge from a Gillette Mach 3 cartridge. In the light of day, my need took on a more artistic posture. The plan was to get professionally branded. An asterisk entry wound and exit wound, burned and blistered into my side to match Dad's scar. In the meantime, I made bracelets from the shoelaces I wore when carrying him. One still had a little bit of blood on it, and that helped.

BLUE. GREY. OLIVE. THE 1940s. My brother Nick once painted a portrait of the young Bill "Pete" Counter on the deck of a ship, a young man who lied about his age to enlist in the navy. Having twice escaped a sinking ship in battle, he was a lieutenant by the time he came home.

My family has many stories from World War II. About Uncle Bob, who was a radio operator in the army. About Grandma, a war nurse for the Allies who attended to Axis soldiers who would scream at her as she cared for them. About my maternal grandparents in occupied Netherlands, and Grandad's time stationed there. But there is no more iconic story than the sniper shot that could have annihilated our family. Young Grandad, a lifelong smoker, was tapping his pipe on a glass ashtray when a rifle bullet blew it out of his hand. The end. We don't know what happened before the shot, or afterward. Just setting, action, interruption.

As far as I know, Grandad didn't have any war scars. No knife wounds or bullet wounds or battlefield amputations. He'd cut off the tip of his thumb accidentally, after the war, working with power tools as a carpenter. And he had a bad back near the end of his life, necessitating a cane and then a walker. But the ashtray was the most visceral proof he was part of the twentieth century's big violent story. A souvenir bearing a scar meant for his body. A heavy piece of glass, no longer functional as a smoking accessory, stored with the rest of the belongings he left behind in death.

RED ON WHITE. Like a peppermint candy. This is how the millennium started. Grandad came with us on our first family cruise. The captain looked just like him, but with a darker tan. They wore the same size glasses, had the same posture and grey beard. The captain was also in the navy during the war. We have a picture of them, standing with Mom, Dad, and Nick—everyone posed in formal wear, at the captain's cocktail party. I wasn't there. Feeling antisocial, I stayed in my cabin watching the TV channel they set up to teach passengers how to play casino games. When I look at that photo now, it feels like the captain was taking my place.

Three years later, still in the red-and-white years, Grandad died in a hospital bed. In his final days, going mad in the intensive care unit after multiple heart attacks, he intermittently lapsed into old memories and thought the war was on again. When I think of these episodes, the colours of time collide. Blue and grey and olive and red and white. The forties warping around the early aughts. I see glimpses of that temporal colour, imagining his state of mind, simultaneously in the present and the past—a one-man Möbius loop. Billy Pilgrim, unstuck in time.

At some point in the post-tangle years, after my timeline withered into its current gossamer state, Mom and I were talking about my struggles with PTSD and bipolar II. She said that when Grandad was alive, she asked him if he or Grandma had any sort of mental effects from the war. He denied it. Dad doesn't have PTSD either, and he's the one who got shot. But I wonder sometimes if synesthesia is hereditary. I wonder if Grandad was time sick like me. And in his final moments, flickering back and forth across the decades, I wonder what colours he saw.

GOTTA DO IT (KILL BABY HITLER)

IF YOU ARE READING THIS, Jeb Bush has failed to go back in time and assassinate baby Hitler. And for whatever reason that might be—the impossibility of time travel, the unalterable nature of the past, general incompetence—it's not for lack of conviction. During the Republican primary election leading up to the 2016 presidential race, while riding a campaign bus through New Hampshire, the second oldest of George H. W. Bush's six children was asked if he would kill the infant that would one day grow into the face of ultimate historical evil.

"Hell yeah, I would," said the man who fought Donald Trump for the opportunity to be the forty-fifth president of the United States of America and lost. "The problem with going back in history and doing that is—as we know from the series *Back to the Future*—it could have a dangerous effect on everything else. But I'd do it. I mean: Hitler."

Robert Zemeckis's 1985 adventure film *Back to the Future*

isn't about murdering baby villains, but Jeb's right to be concerned. When charismatic Marty McFly, played by Michael J. Fox, travels back in time in a modified DeLorean DMC-12, he finds himself interfering in his parents' relationship, accidentally preventing the events that led to his own conception. McFly races through the past, playing matchmaker for his mom and dad, and re-engineering their union and his own birth. But when he returns to the present, he finds things aren't how he left them. His parents are more confident and healthier, the mall has a new name, and Marty's father's adult bully, Biff, has lost his angry edge.

There are many conceptions of time and how traversing it might work from a historical standpoint, but Jeb referencing *Back to the Future* gives us insight into his temporal paradigm. Jeb sees time as a singular series of events that, if changed in the past, rewrite those that come in the future. If he drove back to 1889 in a DeLorean and killed baby Hitler, then returned to his home time, Jeb thinks he would see a world in which the Holocaust didn't happen. It's an act of heroism, no doubt (albeit an impossible one that trivializes one of the greatest atrocities of the twentieth century). And he's on the majority side of the popular opinion—the heroic infanticide question was posed to him because it was the subject of a *New York Times* poll in which 42 percent of respondents said they would kill little Adolf.

At first blush, the baby Hitler hypothetical is merely an edgier, higher-stakes version of the trolly problem in ethics: would you kill one person (or a little baby) to prevent the deaths of five people (or the Holocaust)? But because we are dealing with a fragile line of cause and effect over the span of a century, the equation changes. To kill baby Hitler is to destroy history as we know it, and everyone and everything we know that was created in the wake of his atrocious adulthood.

My paternal grandparents were both World War II veterans. It defined who they were as young adults and how they met in the conflict's aftermath. Without Hitler, there is very little chance that I come to exist. And even if I do, World War II and all its horrors have had such a profound influence on arts, culture, politics, and society that the Peter Counter from a Hitler-less timeline is different enough to be unrecognizable from the person writing these words. I am loath to admit it, but Hitler is a load-bearing monstrosity, historically speaking. An alternate life path carved out of a different social, cultural, and political landscape is akin to annihilation. Death by a thousand choices. I haven't experienced the history Jeb would erase, but everything that shaped the world I was born into is an integral part of who I am.

Consider the television show *Fringe*, a sci-fi procedural modelled after *The X-Files*, but instead of concerning itself with UFOs and government conspiracies, it's about an alternate universe built from the choices we didn't make. In this neighbouring timeline, we re-meet the main characters we've come to love through their misfit chemistry and weekly forensic hijinks—FBI agent Olivia Dunham; her boss, special agent Phillip Broyles; psychedelic mad scientist Walter Bishop—played by the same actors, but burdened with different lives. Sure, in the alternate universe of *Fringe*, some people we know to be dead are alive (the charismatic agent Charlie Francis) and vice versa (Olivia's sister), but more importantly, everyone in both universes is radically distinct from their alternate counterpart. Biologically, the other Oliva is the same as the Agent Dunham we are familiar with, but her life, informed by the alternate world of events both big (9/11 happened differently, the city of Boston was eaten by a wormhole) and small (alternate Oliva has dyed red hair and bangs), makes her a different person all together.

When the alternate version of Broyles sacrifices himself to save regular universe Olivia's life in season 3, it's sad because we know he is a good-hearted person, but seeing his charred corpse is more uncanny than tragic. The prime-universe Broyles whom we've known since the first episode sees the body, learns about the other man's history, and becomes mournful for the life he personally never had but can imagine as almost his—a life where he never divorced, in which he was a good father, and where 9/11 left the Twin Towers standing but levelled the White House.

Fringe's brilliance lies in how it so effortlessly illustrates our vital relationship with history. To make a different choice is to prevent a billion different potential versions of yourself from seeing the light of day, while also affirming your own identity. Our choices are informed by our past— the quotidian and historical, the beautiful, the mundane, and the atrocious. In an alternate world where JFK lived to become ambassador to the United Nations, the characters of *Fringe* are completely different humans. In a world where Jeb Bush kills baby Hitler, you and I don't exist as we do today. Which effectively means we don't exist at all.

It's all quite dramatic on the level of major historical hypotheticals, but this conundrum is at the core of all personal regret and tragedy. Studying harder, partying less, not compromising on our dreams—what if, informed by our experience, we went back to our pasts and made a different choice in order to correct our lives? Would we really replace ourselves with a stranger in our own skin?

I often think about the alternate realities that might have stemmed from wearing a different T-shirt on December 27, 2006. As my dad and I walked in the direction of the pier where he would be shot, we paused at a fork in the road. We could turn right and go back to the ship, or we could continue straight ahead and check out the view of the ocean from the landing just beyond the municipal building on our laser-printed map. An antsy dread grew in me as I looked between the possible destinations, but I glanced down at my shirt, a black graphic tee that Dad bought me as a souvenir at the first karate tournament I ever won. Adorned with silhouettes of martial artists holding various stances in front of a Canadian flag, I treated the shirt like a wearable trophy. *Even if something bad happens*, I thought, *I'm prepared. I know karate.*

Would we have gone back to the ship if I'd worn my White Stripes band tee with the pandas, or a blue Old Navy polo? The vacation would have continued, I would have spent my day reading *Chuck Klosterman IV* as I overcaffein-ated in the ship's café, and I wouldn't be typing this sentence sixteen years later. Every day since the encounter with the gunman on the pier, I've thought about saving my dad's life. The feeling of dread at that crossroads was the subject of myriad therapy sessions, all of which shaped my sense of self. I wouldn't have needed that therapist in the first place had I not stood on that wooden pier where I watched a bullet pierce Dad's chest. In my moments of nostalgic regret, I fantasize about another life defined by different clothes. But if I were to commission Jeb Bush to make a detour on his way to kill Hitler and steal my karate shirt from my luggage—or perhaps to go back further and register in the karate tournament and defeat me by such a margin that it decimates my confidence—I would be bankrolling my own self-annihilation.

I think Jeb knows this, if not with deep nuance then at least on an instinctual level. Could the Bush dynasty exist in a world without Hitler? Certainly not in any recognizable way. But maybe that's the point. Maybe Jeb doesn't want to exist. And maybe he'd take us all with him. He's certainly committed to his baby-killing instincts. When asked to confirm his stance on future tyrant infanticide, he tweeted, "Gotta do it."

The existence of this essay proves Jeb can't do it. Time-travel child murder is beyond his ability, just as impossible for him as inspiring the hearts and minds of the Republican Party. But if his convictions hold, and somehow he finds a way back to the birth of evil, the words on this page might begin to fade, like the face of Marty McFly in his family photos as his meddling with the timeline slowly erases him from space-time. This essay can't exist if Jeb succeeds, and neither can we. Until then, let this ink serve as a canary in Jeb's demented coal mine—a testament to his failure and a reason to celebrate the full spectrum of our lives. The grief, the pain, the regret. Sometimes it's what you can't accomplish that makes you worth toasting.

HEROES

IN A HOUSE ON the shore of the Upper Rideau, in the dead of a forty-below winter night, I might as well have been sitting in a tin can far above the world. A fire glowed in the stove, painting the basement a deep, pulsing red. A colour I associate with the dying light at the end of the universe, the last red dwarf burning out in the void. Dad lay on the couch, eyes closed. I sat in a chair nearby, plucking at an acoustic guitar.

Mom and Nick would arrive the next day. The rest of the house was empty, save for the dog, a black flat-coated retriever named Cheerio. Dad and I had been drinking. And like all times when I am alone with my father, I felt an overwhelming sense of our history together. It's a heavy emotional state for me, and it can make conversation difficult after a certain hour. So I played music. A song about family, and memory, and life, and death, with easy chords and a melody in my lower vocal range. I strummed and quietly sang about forgetting what my mother said, and what my brother said, and what my father said. About having seven days to live my life and seven days to die.

"Did you write that?" Dad asked, stirring on the couch.

"No," I said. "That's a Bowie song."

IF YOU DON'T KNOW how to say something, say it with Bowie. Over his fifty-year career, the king of glam gave us twenty-six studio albums containing every genre of rock this side of nu metal. He sang about everything. Love and fear, pain and ecstasy. Recovery. Reconciliation. Addiction. Being a young dude, liking George Orwell, wanting to abduct magic babies. If you can feel it, Bowie has cooed, squealed, or crooned it.

The rich tradition of imitating Bowie demonstrates how adept he was at voicing our most nuanced emotions. Cover versions of his music range from the iconic (The Wallflowers' "Heroes" from the *Godzilla* soundtrack and G-Eazy's version of "Lazarus"), to the heartbreakingly weird (Karen O and Willy Nelson's "Under Pressure") to the devastatingly unlistenable (Ozzy Osbourne's "All the Young Dudes"). Astronaut Chris Hadfield covered "Space Oddity" on the International Space Station. In the midst of a rare and singular experience, the spaceman turned to Bowie when it came time to express himself.

If I'm ever having an exceptionally far out day, it can feel as if his music underpins all of reality. Once, during a visit to the local occult shop, the witch behind the counter sang the entirety of "Sound and Vision" to herself, not stopping once even as she sold me a Ouija planchette enamel pin. When I wear that accessory over my heart, I find myself humming the electric-blue tune.

An art-school-trained mime by trade, Bowie blended his music with theatre, releasing new characters with his albums, personas he embodied when playing the songs. The alien Ziggy Stardust, the dystopian wasteland rocker Halloween Jack, the dangerous Thin White Duke, the Earthling, and the Blind Prophet—these are only some of the ones with names. Even when he was ostensibly being himself, a sense of theatre pervaded Bowie's presence. He was as much a performer as a musician. As a fan, when you sing "Rock 'n' Roll Suicide" at karaoke, or play "Seven" in the glow of a winter fire, you aren't only putting words to a melody, you are donning a persona. Each song an imitation; we become Bowie.

WHEN I THINK ABOUT DAD, I think about weather. In the 1990s, he was a lineman, and if the lights went out, he answered the call to restore power. High winds. Cold rain. Thunder. When the ice storm of 1998 froze eastern Ontario and southern Quebec for weeks, killing thirty-five people and injuring thousands more, Dad went forth into the January darkness.

My father was always larger than life to me. I think most parents are when you're ten. Perfectly articulate, a generous volunteer, a skilled craftsman who built chairs, swings, and backyard tree forts. Sometimes he was quiet and distant and carried gloom. Other times he was bright and exciting, a perpetual positivity machine who could do anything. He helped me write my first school speech and taught me how to build a circuit. Whenever I pour a glass of water, I remember him helping me with a science project. "Water is a universal solvent," he said. "That's why it's so important in chemistry."

In 1998, when he was away for weeks in the frozen wasteland, I began to imagine him as a hero. A human against the gods. Rescuing families from the icy grip of our planet's fury. When he returned, I started noticing his uncanny connection to nature. On the eve of a snowstorm, he'd stand at the back door of the house and peer into the night sky as if reading hidden messages on the clouds. With near-perfect accuracy he'd tell us if the school buses would be cancelled the next morning.

"If they're not, you can stay home anyway," he'd promise.

Sitting at the kitchen table, listening to my parents' CDs with the TV news on mute, I was introduced to Bowie. Ziggy played guitar while Dad predicted the weather. When I think of Dad, I think of those stormy nights. Not his shooting, but his mythic character. On the streets of Limon, I felt like I was in his world of heightened stakes and primal emotions. Sometimes I wonder if he wasn't traumatized afterward because, for him, getting shot wasn't all that out of place. Just another day in the life of a legend. Barely worth mentioning over dinner.

ALASKA. THE BERING SEA. A submarine glides through the darkness. It jettisons a torpedo with a man in it, and when it reaches Shadow Moses Island, he abandons the projectile and surfaces. A nuclear facility. The terrorist group FOXHOUND has taken hostages and is demanding the remains of the legendary war hero Big Boss. The torpedo man climbs onto cold land and slinks to a safe place, where he receives a two-way call through his private CODEC communicator.

"This is Snake," he says. The protagonist of *Metal Gear Solid*, Solid Snake is a master of the sneaking mission. Able to use any weapon he procures on site and fluent in close-quarters combat, Snake prefers evasion. He's witty, if a bit too serious. Snake is cool and capable, and smokes cigarettes despite the surgeon general's warning. Most importantly, unlike most video game protagonists, he's aiming for the lowest possible kill count. Extreme mode, the game franchise's highest level of difficulty, demands full invisibility—get seen by an enemy and it's game over.

Snake is legendary to me like my dad is legendary to me. I was introduced to Snake as a child and he seemed to exist on a plane of unobtainable adulthood. The sci-fi espionage scenarios of *Metal Gear Solid* seemed as real as my vision of Dad's heroic deeds in the ice storm. Specialized, life saving.

There is a tacit, biological imperative for a son to grow into a facsimile of his father. This theme of succession is at the very core of *Metal Gear Solid* and its many sequels. Late in the first game, Solid Snake learns that he and the leader of FOXHOUND—Liquid Snake—are brothers, results of a secret "Les Enfants Terribles" government project to clone the ultimate warrior Big Boss. The intention was to literally have the sons become new versions of the father. It didn't work out as planned, the brothers fought it out on Shadow Moses Island, Solid Snake killed Liquid, and the world was safe from nuclear disaster. For the time being.

Hideo Kojima, the creator of *Metal Gear*, is a visionary game director who spends decades exploring his pet themes. A topic as rich as intergenerational identity took him more than twenty-five years. In the second *MGS* entry, subtitled *Sons of Liberty*, Kojima forces players to contend with the distance between generations, making Solid Snake a non-playable character and introducing a new protagonist, Raiden. Raiden has all of Snake's moves, all of Snake's weapons, and has effectively been brainwashed to be Snake. On top of all that, the mission is so similar to the Shadow Moses incident from the first game that the characters frequently comment on it. In the third entry, *Snake Eater*, the franchise goes full-on ouroboros and casts player one as Big Boss—the ostensible beginning of the legacy—on a sneaking mission in the 1960s. His code name is Snake, and he has Snake's voice and face. If you weren't paying attention to the game's infamously long dialogue scenes, you could be tricked into thinking this *was* Snake. In the fourth game, *Guns of the Patriots*, you return to Solid Snake, but now he is Old Snake, according to the name above your health bar, and because two-thirds of the franchise has been dedicated to other people, it's hard to remember who Solid Snake is by now. This is compounded by Kojima's choice to lessen the incentive to be non-lethal, giving the player a choice: Do you really care about Solid Snake enough to be Solid Snake again? Because you don't have to.

Throughout my teens and twenties, as new *Metal Gear Solid* sequels were released, I saw parts of Dad in my face when I looked in the mirror, and I felt the same swings of emotions from my inherited mood disorder. When we experienced gun violence together, on the day he was shot, I felt bonded to him in a way that I can best describe as successive. I carried Dad to safety because that's the kind of thing Dad would do. We're not the same person, but we have the same blood. We have the same history.

The final entry in Kojima's *Metal Gear Solid* games, *The Phantom Pain*, ties all these threads of identity together—the context of the story, how you choose to play, and who you believe you are. By far the longest and most expansive of the *Metal Gear Solid* games, *The Phantom Pain* places you once again in an idea of Snake. You play dozens of hours under the pretext that you are Big Boss in 1984. But if you manage to uncover a hidden audio tape, the truth is revealed: you're not Big Boss. You're just some guy. Punished Snake, as the character is called, was in a helicopter crash with the real Big Boss, then surgically altered to look like him. Through circumstances out of his control, he was asked, "What would Big Boss do?" and in doing so became indistinguishable from the original model.

Given his complex understanding of identity, it should come as no surprise that Hideo Kojima is a massive David Bowie fan. It's easy to focus on the speculative espionage intrigue and Byzantine historical fiction of the *Metal Gear Solid* franchise, but part of its enduring appeal is its style. From the skin-tight clothing and chic hair styles, to the hyperviolence and fetishization of nationalist icons, to character designs and names lifted straight out of a moonage daydream, *Metal Gear* is glam. And no game is more glam than *The Phantom Pain*, which is essentially a hundred-hour celebration of David Bowie's Orwellian sci-fi concept album *Diamond Dogs*.

The details are meticulous and deserving of their own book—how without the use of any *Diamond Dogs* tracks, Kojima is able to turn an audio experience into a ludic one through aesthetic choices and motifs—but one Bowie detail in *The Phantom Pain* stands out more than others. The game is bookended with the song "The Man Who Sold the World." But here's the kicker: it's a cover by Midge Ure. The real Bowie, just like Big Boss himself, is missing in action.

Snake, like Bowie, is an aspirational identity. Something amorphous and playful. A way we express ourselves. And if we don the identity of our heroes—put on the makeup, wear the eye patch, move and speak the way legends do—it doesn't matter if we are physically distinct. The truth of who we are in relationship to one another is defined by the feedback loop of imitation. I follow my father's example and know him in the ways my performance deviates from his script.

I PREFER DOLPHINS AND my brother prefers sharks. I always saw my dad in my brother—an affinity for team sports, strong opinions, infectious gregariousness. Nick's middle name is our Dad's first name and they were both small as kids. Both are more naturally aggressive than me and understand competitive principles better. So I assumed my father also preferred sea dogs. But Dad liked dolphins too. I could hear the wonder in his voice when we watched a Robin Williams Discovery Channel special about dolphins, and he loves the song "Heroes" by David Bowie, in which dolphins embody freedom.

Christmas morning, 2006, we docked in Costa Maya, Mexico. Dad and I ate a quick breakfast, then disembarked from the *Liberty* and boarded a shuttle bus that ferried us from the port, across bumpy roads though expansive yellow-green mangroves. The sky fluctuated between brilliant sun and a high-UV overcast that felt like a white computer screen with the brightness turned up to the max. We stepped off the bus in the parking lot of a Delphinus facility.

According to the marine wildlife experts who outfitted us with life jackets, the dolphins they worked with were not technically in captivity. They can come and go as they please, but they have learned that if they respond to sonar pings around showtimes they get a free meal in the safety of the open-door enclosures. There were about a dozen tourists in all, and we filed onto the docks that surrounded two dolphin pools—squared-off areas of the coast with openings for the animals to swim through.

In that moment of anticipation, waiting for a dolphin to answer the inaudible dinner bell, my mind slipped into a fit of free association. The impossible cavernous levels of *Ecco the Dolphin* rendered in sixteen-bit graphics for the Sega Genesis, and the surreal images of its time-travelling sci-fi sequel. The soft fuzz of the plush dolphin I slept with instead of a teddy bear as a child. The muscle memory of the dolphin kick—a swimming stroke I learned when I was eleven, taking private lessons from my neighbour who was a lifeguard. A chorus of Bowies, wishing they could swim, like dolphins can swim.

The dolphin entered the enclosure like a grey torpedo and swam circles around the perimeter. Its clicking and squealing sounded alien, and the physicality of the creature felt strange. These animals have played a role in our culture since antiquity, memorialized in the constellations of stars in the sky. And yet encounters are so rare as to feel elevated and holy. The dolphin was, in this sense, a cosmic presence.

As a group, we treaded water in a large circle as the dolphin, Yaaj, swam around, underneath, and between us—clicking and squealing, jumping out of the water. We climbed out of the pool, and then each of us had a photo opportunity. The animal's intelligence felt apparent to me, and I got the impression it was treating this like a theatrical performance. Yaaj was an actor performing a residency and taking photos with fans for smelts. I splashed the water and held my arms out in a wide circle, which Yaaj swam through to make it look like we were old friends embracing. On Dad's turn, he held his arm out, Frankenstein style, and Yaaj lifted herself out of the water vertically to give the illusion they were holding hands (or fins) and dancing. The photograph captures the most unguarded and genuine smiles each of us has ever taken. You can see the relation: I inherited my father's unrestrained joy.

After the encounter, we lounged on a beach and a man served us spiced rum in plastic cups. I sat on the sand and stared at the horizon as Dad waded into the water. Shrinking in the distance until I only saw his head. Day-drunk and euphoric, I felt like I understood Dad better than ever before. A man in commune with the environment. And forty-eight hours later, feeling the warmth of his blood, I'd know him as truly elemental.

FINE

FINE IS THE GREAT NULLIFIER. All of life's experiences fit onto a spectrum of positive and negative, and fine is always zero. It orients itself at the fulcrum of the experiential scale. On either end are the hypothetical what-ifs and if-onlys. Fantasy best- and worst-case scenarios, unachievable dreams and impossible nightmares. To move forward without burdening our friends and family and the expectation of our demanding capitalist society, we balance the scales and situate our personal happenings in the middle. It could always be better, we say, keeping ourselves hungry for progress. It could have been worse, we say, dividing our pain by nothing. Someone could have died. Everything turned out fine.

We explore the negative end of the experiential spectrum in dark fantasy, speculative fiction, and horror. Novelist Kim Newman shows the extent of this recentring effect in the second entry in his Anno Dracula series, *The Bloody Red*

Baron. Anno Dracula imagines an alternate reality based on two simple premises: first, what if *Dracula* were a historical account, but instead of being slain by Van Helsing's hunting party, the count successfully conquered the British throne. Second, what if every other public domain genre fiction character, including Lovecraftian mad scientist Herbert West, Sherlock's brother Mycroft Holmes, infamous queer icon conman Tom Ripley, and every vampire you're ever seen in a pre–*Buffy the Vampire Slayer* movie, also existed? The result is an epic alternate history spanning centuries that puts all of our mortal troubles into sharp relief. Famine, war, pestilence, death—it's all unspeakably horrible on its own. But at least there weren't immortal bloodsucking monsters making it worse.

While Newman explores a wide range of historic atrocities and disasters, from Jack the Ripper to Y2K, it's his take on World War I that wins the It Could Be Worse Award. By Dracula-fying the Great War, he exponentially raises the death toll and amplifies the expendability of young human life. Pouring vampires on the twentieth century's first defining global conflict introduces a new level of insignificance to mortal soldiers, whose lives are antlike when compared to the eternal existences of their enemies. It does nothing to mitigate the very real body horrors of trench foot, mustard gas, and meat-grinder combat, but does add the gothic grotesquery of shape-shifting German ace pilots who morph into gigantic bats that silently glide through the night sky and exsanguinate their enemies.

To the pragmatist, this might sound silly, perhaps even disrespectful. And it is, to an extent. But all fantasy is an affront to genuine experience. Alternate realities grounded in what we understand as natural law and those involving vampires do the same thing: they shift the scope of imaginable possibility, relocating our experience to the axis. Zeroed out, we conclude our life could have been worse.

"CAN YOU BELIEVE THIS?" Dad sipped a can of Budweiser as we both sat under the orange-and-raspberry-sherbet sky, legs stretched out on pool chairs, a bucket of beer between us, on the Lido Deck of the *Liberty*.

"This could be worse," I said. "This could be a lot worse."

It had been a day of firsts. My first time in Costa Rica, my first look at a revolver, my first gunshot. My first saved life, my first police lineup, my first judge. My first victim report and now my first beer with Dad. We'd had beers around one another before, with the rest of the family, but never in this cliché, father-son bonding sort of way. Given the events of the day, it almost never happened. Had he died on the pier, in the street, or lying in the ship's medical bay, I'd be having a different kind of drink.

"We have some luck," Dad said. "Starting the day like that and ending up here."

I laughed. My body was simultaneously numb with exhaustion and vibrating at high alert. I sipped my beer and fixated on my shoe. Near my right pinky toe, two dark spots stared back at me: errant drops of Dad's blood I'd failed to sop up with the green hoodie I used to staunch the hole in his side during our long walk. The rest of the evidence camouflaged—Dad's bandaged wound disappeared under a fresh black T-shirt, my gore-covered sweater and jeans were taken from me to be cleaned by the ship's crew, our adrenalin-fuelled giddiness matched the Lido Deck's happy hour vibe of sun-drunk euphoria. Nick and Mom, running late on their zipline tour, would have no reason to believe we did anything but lounge around the ship all day.

"We can keep this just between us," Dad said.

I laughed again. *Why not?* I thought. *What's the point of going into the details? Everything turned out fine.*

INVENTORY

Shoebox for size 10½ dress shoes
The box was forest green when it served its initial purpose, holding a pair of black shoes I bought to wear at my first barista job. It's the perfect size for collecting miscellanea, so I kept it to store the ephemeral bits and bobs I can never bring myself to part with. Playbills, pins, watches that froze and I haven't fixed. Ticket stubs, collectable cards for defunct games, key cards from cruise vacations, old letters from people whose names I would forget had they not written it under "sincerely." The carbon copy of a police report. A belt now flimsy from wear. Stuff that is otherwise easy to lose or mistake for trash. Call me an emotional pack rat, but the box's contents are as precious to me as they are eclectic.

   Under the box's lid, its colour now faded to dusty grey after years of moving between apartments and houses and cities, the bric-a-brac collects. Each item is a viewfinder sharpening the definition of life's notable moments, revealing the spiderweb details that are so fragile and easy to sweep up. The broad strokes and showcase events are easy for me to recall without aid, but it's the fine ornamentation—the specific language, the typos, the serial numbers—that make it so valuable.

I opened the shoebox yesterday to add a burned DVD to the memorial pile. I found the silver disc in a basement storage bin, and it contains videos of martial arts techniques for use in at-home practice, recorded by Shihan, the karate master of the dojo where I got my black belt. The disc shines among the odd and ends, its imbued memories resonating with the other souvenirs. With every addition, my time capsule defies the laws of entropy. The messier it gets, the more order I see; a galaxy of personal history coalescing from dust.

Triple Triad *playing card*
A playing card from the 1999 marketing campaign for the video game *Final Fantasy VIII*. A thin gold border frames the image of a grey-haired woman in a blue shirt. She has an eye patch. A man with baggy pants and a vest over his bare chest stands behind her. They're holding arcane weapons and strike a confrontational pose. Fujin and Raijin, minor boss enemies in the game, turned into a trading card. The flipside is the exact same but with a red background. The numbers two, eight, eight, and four are printed in the top-left corner. These are the card's stats in case you somehow know anyone else with physical *Triple Triad* cards.

Triple Triad is a minigame in *Final Fantasy VIII*, an epic Japanese roleplaying game for PlayStation that sees six military high school students travelling to the edge of time and space in order to preserve their memories of each other by defeating the evil sorceress Ultimecia. Their adventure takes them into the past, present, and far future. From the heart of a volcano, to the bottom of the sea, to the centre of international wars, to within spitting distance of the monster-infested moon. It's a phantasmagorical journey filled with thrilling violence and sweeping teen melodrama. But for all its operatic set pieces and entertaining battles, to many players the most memorable parts of *Final Fantasy VIII* involve playing cards.

I'd estimate about one in every five non-player characters you encounter in *Final Fantasy VIII* will drop everything they are doing, even in the middle of an apocalyptic event or military invasion, to play cards with you if you press the square button near them. The card game is easy to learn, difficult to master, and played with a deck you build throughout your adventure—winning cards from boss fights, stealing them from monsters, or receiving them as gifts from the game's supporting cast. *Triple Triad* cards vary in rarity within the game, and many are one of a kind. Those bearing the likeness of *Final Fantasy VIII*'s dramatis personae are particularly powerful on the card table, and are exceedingly difficult to acquire. That said, playing *Triple Triad* is entirely optional, and your cards in the game cannot be traded or used to play with other *Final Fantasy VIII* players. It's a closed system. Unless you have the physical counterpart, like the Fujin and Raijin card that resides in my shoebox.

Final Fantasy VIII was a blockbuster, and its publisher, Squaresoft, promoted it by physically printing every digital *Triple Triad* card from the game, selling them in foil packs in the style of *Magic: The Gathering* or *Pokémon* cards.

Throughout the fall of 1999, my brother and I saved up our allowances for weeks, hauled stacks of loonies and toonies to the Stone Road Mall Electronics Boutique, and built our meagre *Triple Triad* decks one pack at a time. We played the game together on the living room coffee table, bringing our favourite virtual world to life in the smallest way. The magic and time travel romance of *Final Fantasy VIII* was confined to our imaginations, but the culture of that distant world felt real because we could hold a small part of it in our hands.

The physical *Triple Triad* cards received a limited printing. Now the only way to build a deck is through online auction houses, where they are sold by the fifteen-pack box for about five thousand dollars. The digital *Triple Triad* cards have value in the game too. Each one can be transmogrified into rare materials and magic that come in handy during the video game's exceedingly difficult final hours. You can open the menu, browse your collection of digital cards, and choose to irreversibly transform them from unique tokens into consumable resources meant for combat rather than play. Devastatingly powerful pulse ammo, Ultima magic that can exponentially increase a character's fighting power, and an item that grants temporary invulnerability—these resources, in the quantities refined from your card, are just as difficult to obtain, but they can't be used to play *Triple Triad*. And you can't reverse the process.

In my four or five playthroughs of *Final Fantasy VIII*, I have never refined a rare *Triple Triad* card for its powerful consumable items, for the same reason I still have my physical Fujin and Raijin. I can't shake the sense of loss I might feel, which is more of an anticipatory worry than an informed caution. What if I need it later for an important battle? Or, more important: what if by using it up or discarding it for keeps, I forget the small details that give the game's grand arcs their texture? The numbers in the corner, the position of Fujin's eye patch, the weight of the coins in my wallet. Time spent with my brother, rubbed off on a piece of cardstock. That's the point of these games, after all—to treasure the characters and the story. Otherwise, what is all the violence and drama for?

Three mag-stripe key cards

IMPORTANT THIS IS YOUR SAIL AND SIGN CARD
This card should be kept with you at all times during your cruise and whenever leaving the vessel. You will be required to present this card to re-board the ship. A suggested 15% gratuity will automatically be added to all bar purchases unless otherwise noted. Minimum drinking age is 21. Lost cards should be reported to the Purser's Office immediately.

Two of the cards are blue, with splashes of red and white. One is gold. All three have the same disclaimer on the back. One card says DESTINY in the top-right corner on the front. The other two say LIBERTY. Momentous names for vessels by any measure. The key to my cabin door and my ticket to drinking at the bar. I had no trouble buying alcohol with my LIBERTY card as a nineteen-year-old cruise passenger, despite the Sail and Sign pledge.

It would be more poetic if the card labelled DESTINY was

associated with my father's shooting, but it's the LIBERTY cards that were with me on that day. Other than my passport, they were the only items in my pockets. I remember the wood-veneered kiosk where I had to insert the gold card to get back onto the ship, and the digital chime it elicited when it validated my entry. When I hold the LIBERTY cards, I feel the energy drain from my muscles, sapped by a deep exhaustion from out of time.

Ticket for the Hunter Karate Academy 2004 Black Belt Spectacular

A blue rectangle of card stock featuring the graphic of a karate-ka in a kokutsu dachi performing an open-hand gaiden barai and age uke. Next to him is the address of the public high school auditorium where I was presented with my black belt on November 27, 2004. Weeks prior, I had completed a gruelling two-day gauntlet, starting on the grey mats of the dojo, which I seasoned with my sweat, tears, and blood, before moving to Shihan's forested property outside of town where I learned to break personal limitations with the power of a kiai. The Black Belt Spectacular was a celebration and showcase of the six candidates that year who ascended to the next level of martial arts training. Our white uniforms glowing under blacklight, we performed a kata on a stage to music of our choice. I picked "Somebody to Love" by Jefferson Airplane.

The Black Belt Spectacular tickets cost five dollars. The one I kept was stamped with the number 189 in black ink. My friends and family attended. It was the proudest moment of my young life. I performed two tornado kicks and punched through wooden boards. Shihan said he was proud before replacing my final colour belt with the heavier black sash. We bowed, shook hands, and he hugged me.

After receiving my black belt, my endorphins triggered my yet-to-be-diagnosed bipolar II. Driving my mom's purple Acura through a fog of hypomania to meet with Shihan and the rest of my martial arts friends for a celebratory dinner at the local Kelsey's, I almost merged lanes into another car. The woman behind the wheel of her red sedan honked at me and screamed. I laughed and cried at the same time, alone if not safe in the solitude of the car. I never told anyone about that close call, but the memory is in the ticket.

Black leather belt
Mom and Dad gave me a black leather belt for Christmas the year I started high school. It came coiled in a white box. During the week, I wore it with my school uniform—white oxford shirt, plaid tie, black slacks, dress shoes—every day for years. On weekends, it held up my jeans and corduroys.

One day when I was seventeen, I pulled the belt off in a single fluid motion and wrapped it around my neck. Using the wooden post of my twin bed for leverage, I strangled the vision from my eyes. I heard my blood struggle through my arteries. My heart pumped and lungs strained to suck air. It sounded like the compression of packing snow. Muted crunching.

Slipping into suffocating darkness, I loosened the belt. It was guilt that saved me. How dare I leave a dead teen in the bedroom where my family expected to find a son and brother? Then came the crisis therapy, and the psychiatry, and the bipolar diagnosis, and my parents' support. I wore the belt the next day. And I wore it the day after that, and after that too. I wore that belt to my high school graduation, I wore it to class in university, and I wore it as I approached the guard rail of the wooden pier in Costa Rica where Dad would be shot. Self-conscious of how my skinny legs looked in shorts, I'd decided to wear jeans that day. The belt kept my pants from falling down as I carried my father to safety.

Police report

A tiny rectangle of carbon paper unfolds into a document titled Organismo de Investigación Judicial Acta de Secuestro. A blue ink seal authenticates it as an official document of the Delegacion Regional O.I.J. I Circuito Judicial Zona Atlantica. Stamped in red ink, we have the case number: "No. 350239."

The rest of the paper is a morbid mad lib, the answers fading on the page despite years of safekeeping. It's still legible, and by closely inspecting the cursive writing, you can discern the precinct (OIJ Limon), the time the document was created (13:05), the date (27 Decembre de 2006), and for some reason, the name of the cruise ship after the Spanish word for "bank" (Banco *Carnivale Liberty*). My name precedes a one-sentence description of the shooting. Three squiggly lines void the remaining ruled space for observaciones.

At the bottom of the paper are four names and signatures. Alex, Carlos, Lir—the commissioner and two witnesses. Next to the label "interesado" is my own name, printed in jagged adrenalin-spiked chicken scratch. In the bottom-left corner someone wrote "N Mora" in black ballpoint pen. I have no idea what that means.

The increasingly illegible nature of the report makes for a grievous metaphor. Even souvenirs degrade. But I'm not disturbed by the fading account of Dad's shooting. I can't speak or read Spanish without help from an app, and the date and time are already seared into my synapses, so the data is less important to me than the aura of the document. Proof that my memories are founded in tangible reality. Yes, I was there in Limon when my father was shot. Here is my piece of carbon paper to prove it.

Letter

I keep the police report safe in an envelope with my name written on it in blue pen. The envelope also contains a letter I received from a mentor and friend after the black belt exam. The author was vying for her third-degree black belt. My eye was set on first degree. And while we trained together as 2004 black belt candidates, her grading demanded she meet the first-degree candidates in opposition during the two-day assessment. Conducting the onslaught, she forced us to find our weakest points and work through them. It felt like a dramatic betrayal at the time, but like everything involved with the black belt process, it was composed purposefully as a way to make each one of us confront our loneliest, most hopeless places and climb out of them.

"I did not like seeing you at your weakest point," she wrote. "But we both know this experience has prepared you for your future life challenges."

She gave me the letter in person and told me to read it

in private. We were both in our uniforms, black belts tied in perfect square knots. I tucked the envelope in my duffel bag and took it home after class. I read the note alone in my room. I know it meant a lot to me then, to feel the camaraderie with a mentor, that sense of bonding over pain and accomplishment. But I was only seventeen, incapable of understanding the true gravity of her message until I lived more life, collected its debris, appreciated the amount of time it can take to make sense of it all. The games. The vacations. The crises. The victories. Solitary stars, until night grows dark enough to reveal full constellations.

She closed the note with a quotation from Confucius: "It does not matter how slowly you go as long as you do not stop."

THE OPHELIA CONUNDRUM

YOU STOP BREATHING. The belt constricts and darkness creeps in at the edges. The stress ball squeeze of blood pushing through constricted arteries. Taste the air with a paper-dry tongue and a gaping mouth. Imitate a gasp. No oxygen. Panic.

Urgency floods into the suicidal void in your stupid heart, your head fills with images of loved ones and the pain they will feel when they find a body where they expected you, their son, brother, friend. Hate the impulse. Claw at the leather strap, scratching red lines on soft throat skin. Remove the noose, throw it at the closed wooden door. Fall to the floor and cry. You can't even do this right.

"SUICIDE TAKES AN ELEGANT state of mind," said my stagecraft professor. "One must be capable of committing murder and desire to be murdered. Quite something."

It was two years after my bedroom suicide attempt, a year

before my encounter with gun violence. I'd been to two therapists, a psychiatrist, and my family doctor, scored a bipolar II diagnosis, and managed to subdue my suicidal urges without medication. I thought I was an expert in morbid ideation. But my professor's little aside during his lecture on *Hamlet* made everything click. The reason I failed to strangle myself to the great beyond was that I didn't possess the right balance between murderous and self-sacrificial.

My professor's literary analysis made intuitive sense in the way other explanations of my mood disorder never did. Dad called it chemical. My school guidance counsellor called it emotional. Movies and TV presented bipolar and comparable illnesses as metaphysical—the stuff of split personalities and psychological horror. But none of that ever really felt correct. I didn't medicate my brain's imbalance, and comparing it to an emo phase was reductive. The Ophelia conundrum of lethal intent, however, with its logical short-circuit, fit in with my experience. For me, bipolar manifests through the elements of style.

The first-person confessional tone of this book is a refined version of my inner monologue when I am in a lucid neutral mood or hypomanic. On the downswing, when my emotional pendulum enters its dark phase, the pronouns change. No longer I, but you.

The difference between a one-letter word and a three-letter word. A simple search-and-replace, and suddenly inner commentary becomes negative self-talk: dissociation, self-objectification, criticism. The second-person perspective allows for judgment. You are so stupid. Nobody likes you. You have no talent. You have no reason to live. You should

die. Who botches something so simple as a suicide? You
do. Pathetic.

YOU END UP IN Dr. Black's office because you fucked up.
Normally, teenagers don't get this treatment, but you're
exceptional in the worst way. A forest shades the asylum
grounds. Leaves and branches diffuse the sunlight before it
hits the window behind your psychiatrist, washing the room
in gold and green, turning your doctor into a silhouette. For
your whole life, schoolmates made fun of this place. There
was a rumour Michael Jackson stayed at this mental hospital. They pointed at it and spoke in a falsetto, pretended to
moonwalk. You're an outpatient, not a threat to yourself
anymore. Just far enough from sanity to get out of school
once a week to tell a shadowy man you were too hyper
to do your mood homework. Big surprise. All you had to
do was write a stupid number on a calendar. Zero for the
worst depression ever, ten for the best you've ever felt. The
way your mood tracker looks, it's like you don't know any
numbers past six.

And then there are the days on the calendar you left blank.
Days when you knew you didn't have a problem, when life
seemed too beautiful to waste with therapy. They help the
doctor pinpoint how you're defective. You tried to kill yourself; there's really no need to prove you can be depressed.
The gaps in your mood record represent the time you spent
marvelling at life's grand euphorias. Writing terrible songs
on the guitar you can barely play, going for aimless walks in
the forest across the street and getting lost for hours gawking

at nature like a psycho hermit, talking too loud in group settings, embarrassing yourself by being overly familiar with acquaintances. You know they're mocking you for that, right?

Defining the extent of your highs was the hard part. Are you truly manic or simply experiencing hypomania? Do you black out on your upswing, or can you remember every pathetic moment? Dr. Black tells you a story about a truly manic patient who phoned the hospital from a rest stop and left a midnight voice mail. He wanted to say he was cured. He felt great. He was done with psychiatry. He had no time for it, focusing entirely on a new hobby: rollerblading the Trans-Canada Highway. Even you'd never do something so cringeworthy.

In the end, the doctor determines you have bipolar II. So unoriginal. Like preferring a sequel to the original.

"It's a rapid cycle," he says. "I can prescribe medication. But only if you want it."

He tells you the side effects. The weight fluctuations, the appetite stuff, the sleep stuff. There are even more mood swings. Apparently, trying to fix your suicidal moods can cause suicide if you're not careful.

"Can I just get rid of the depression and keep the good parts?"

It doesn't work that way, dummy.

FBI AGENT DALE COOPER is the picture of hypomania. The sunniest disposition in the grimmest circumstances. Coop is the coffee- and pie-loving lawman assigned to solve the gruesome murder of Laura Palmer, a teenager who was sexually assaulted and killed by her demon-possessed father, then wrapped in plastic and dumped in the river. In every episode of David Lynch and Mark Frost's television show *Twin Peaks*, Agent Cooper is surrounded by the deepest evil on our planet, and he smiles in its face, revelling in the town's idiosyncrasies and dispensing positive advice like, "Every day, once a day, give yourself a present. Don't plan it, don't wait for it, just let it happen."

When I'm on the upswing into hypomania, I feel like Agent Cooper. Sunny, optimistic, eager to spread joy and savour life's finest treats. I'm not naive, though. I know about my proclivity for self-harm. I remember the attempts at strangulation, the experimentation with sharp objects, and the shameful self-beatings. But in the upswing state, I can't help but smile. Moments of light and communities of love wash away all but life's worst stains. There is a heroism in darkness-informed positivity. Self-love in the face of atrocity.

Just as light is defined by its contrasting darkness, Agent Cooper is defined by his doppelgänger. A demonic evil twin from the Black Lodge—the jazzy backwards dream palace with zigzag floors and red curtains that helped define *Twin Peaks'* aesthetic. In the Season 2 finale, which aired in 1991, Agent Cooper descends into the lodge and is subdued by his double, who replaces him in the real world. The show took a twenty-six-year hiatus before returning in 2017, and for that entire period, the man with Coop's face was a bad guy.

To those who knew him, Cooper disappeared into darkness. He became the kind of person you pray to never meet. A killer in a leather jacket with black shark eyes. But viewers know that the good guy is still out there, imprisoned in another dimension, waiting until he's allowed to return. In Season 3, the men with identical faces vie for the right to exist in the mortal realm, but they never directly interact. Coop attempts to recover his sunny demeanour and the double schemes to remain in charge of their shared identity. But fate intervenes. The evil Coop is shot dead and Agent Cooper remembers his past life with all its presents.

I find the doppelgänger storyline in *Twin Peaks* painful to watch. To see the havoc wreaked by Coop's double, while the real agent is trapped in a place outside of time, feels like a bipolar switch. Which is not to say my downswing is evil like Coop's double. My depressed self is not dangerous to others. But coming out of a depressive episode does feel like waking up from a bad dream, or returning from the Black Lodge. I am aware of time's passage and I mourn the damage done in the absence of lucidity. I feel the need to fix things.

Unlike PTSD, bipolar II does not have a distinct narrative origin. With my mood disorder, I can't point to an anecdote and say: this event disabled me. My manic depression is a monster with my face, hiding out there in the secret places between trees and dreams. It desires my life and hates me for living it.

The war between Agent Cooper and his doppelgänger is dramatic and emotionally torturous, but it's not the core conflict of *Twin Peaks*. The show features a bipolar allegory, but trauma is at its heart. The series opens on the death of seventeen-year-old Laura Palmer. We are forlorn from the start. When Coop returns to this world after his double dies, he immediately fixates on the loss of Laura, twenty-seven years after her death. He finds a way to travel to the past and prevent the young woman's murder. In his obsession, he is unrecognizable. His personality-defining cheer is replaced by a singular focus on wiping away the most tragic event he's ever known.

Uninhibited by his evil alter ego, Coop attempts to erase the trauma of Laura Palmer's murder from history. He succeeds. But instead of a happy ending—the perpetual hypomania of painless coffee and pie—*Twin Peaks* concludes with a bone-chilling scream. Failure.

If only Coop's optimism had been curbed. If only his fantasy of a less violent life had been criticized in the second person. Our shadow selves are bastards. They're killers and bullies and monsters. But they keep us balanced, locked in a cold war between self-preservation and annihilation, so we remember the price of joy. Understand that in order to kill you, your doppelgänger must also want to die, making every failed attempt an act of self-love. Give yourself a present.

ADVENT

THE SNOW'S COMING DOWN. I'm watching it fall. People all around, their heads twisting in circles, popping off, and floating into the sky. Decapitated bodies, clad in scarves and Canada Goose jackets, falling prone. Scattered shopping bags filled with presents and ribbons, wrapping and tags, tinsel, trimmings, and trappings. Roast beast and Who Hash. It's only a dream. But it bleeds into my waking life once the peppermint lattes and mall Santas come out of hibernation.

My first time in the dream, it took place on my parents' driveway. Strangers slowly trudged up the hill toward me, amassed like zombies, but not shambling. The walkers moved with intelligence and purpose. When they arrived on the front lawn, they attacked. I defended myself with tools from the garage—rakes, shovels, a ski pole—but every implement failed me. One of the mobbers, a man in a suit, pressed forward, immune to my frantic defences. My weapons bent on impact, bounced off his skin, and fell up into the sky. He laughed in my face, his eyes huge and angry. A flash of a blue gun. Was it him? The man who shot Dad? Unsure, I placed my hands on both sides of the suit man's face and twisted. His neck snapped, but he kept laughing, so I kept turning and rotating, around and around. The skin and bones separated like warm Silly Putty and his laughing head floated up, joining the misshapen shovels and crowbars and hacksaws in the sky. Morbid satellites and space trash.

The suited body crumpled to the asphalt as the rest of the crowd advanced. A woman in a salmon dress with a handbag. A man with jeans, a white shirt, and a red baseball cap. Stock characters. Soccer players. Hippies. Cops. A chef in an apron. A doctor. A painter. Their eyes bulging. Laughing as I spun their heads off, clouding the air with hovering skulls. I woke up exhausted, just in time for my retail shift at the fancy mall chocolate store. It was the holiday season and, day after day, the crowds were hostile and unrelenting.

My neck-twisting nightmare imagery doesn't exactly need a Freudian case study. Like most traumatic dreams, the symbols are obvious. The Christmas decor and the overwhelming rush of customer service in December must have triggered my associations. The evergreen, the holly green, the wrapping paper, hostile strangers with red Starbucks cups, Christmas carols—exactly how the world looked in the weeks before Dad's shooting. Steeping the acidic dread that precedes flashbacks and hypervigilance, the holiday season aesthetic primed me for a repeat. The terrible holiday tradition.

The part about the heads, that was weird. That was from someone else's trauma. A few months after our day in Costa Rica, when I was home for a weekend, Dad told me about another family who was attacked in Limon. Halfway up the forested mountain out of town, their shuttle was ambushed by men wielding machetes. The family—a mom, dad, their two daughters, and their grandfather—exited the van. Their attackers made demands. But the grandfather, a combat veteran, snapped into action, disarming the men and killing one by breaking his neck.

I don't know the veracity of this story. Part of me thinks that an altercation involving a murder in self-defence on vacation would be bigger news, but then again, even though a story about Dad appeared on the local news, reports of our mishap didn't travel far. Unbelievable violence happens all the time and bad news is a competitive racket. True or not, the machete ambush stuck with me. So when Advent reminded my amygdala about its new tradition of pain and screaming, I thought of decapitation. My ghost of borrowed Christmas past.

This all might sound tragic and grim, but I'd call it seasonally appropriate. You can't do much better than the lead-up to Christmas for heavy metal horror vibes. The Advent story is practically Cthulian. The darkness, the harsh winter conditions, and the celebratory anticipation of a god taking human form as foretold in ancient texts. A supernatural birth in a barn. Set it in Massachusetts instead of Bethlehem and you're more than halfway to writing *The Dunwich Horror*. If baby Jesus grew to his full size by feasting on raw livestock, gnashing his teeth as his bloated flesh pressed against the straining rafters of the stable—as some gods made incarnate are wont to do—we'd remember H. P. Lovecraft as a Bible nerd instead of a nihilist.

But you don't need blood and guts to creep up Christmas. (Besides, body horror and torture porn are the domain of Easter.) Advent horror is all about signs and wonders, a pervasive sense of doom. Weird stars and hosts of many-winged spectral messengers portending the end of an era. A god is going to be born of a woman because there's too much sin in the world. Something is coming. It's going to be huge.

Imagine standing in the presence of that infant deity on a dark night and trying not to tremble and recoil. This child is of the same essence that destroyed cities and turned people to pillars of salt. The essence was there in the darkness, before light, when the oceans raged indistinguishable from the perpetual night sky, black on black. It commanded the locusts and frogs and bacteria in their siege on Egypt. It banished humanity from Eden, and shortly thereafter flooded the world and killed the unicorns. That thing in the manger may look like a boy, but it's a weapon of mass destruction that in thirty years or so will prove to be unkillable. Really puts all those dream decapitations into perspective.

The coming of the Messiah is the beginning of the Bible's New Testament, which of course means it's the end of the Old Testament. Advent, therefore, is pre-apocalyptic. It's the first story we read on the long and exhausting epistolary road to the Book of Revelations. We celebrate the holiday as we approach the darkest day of December, followed by the new year, which is the death of the old year.

This doomy tone carries through holiday stories beyond the Bible. *Sir Gawain and the Green Knight* is an Arthurian tale filled with pagan symbolism that begins over Christmas feasting in Camelot. The festivities are interrupted by a monstrous green man wielding an axe. He proposes a game: one of the Knights of the Round Table shall land a blow on him, and in a year's time, the attacker will seek out the intruder and have the exact same pain revisited on himself. Sir Gawain, an untested boy, volunteers to play. He lands a decapitating death blow on the interloper. But dread descends on the hall as the Green Knight's body climbs to its feet, retrieves his unattached head, and retreats, filling the night air with wicked laughter. And so begins the terrible annual cycle, revisiting the violence of Christmases past.

Karma is the name of the game when it comes to the supernatural scariness of Christmastime. In Charles Dickens's *A Christmas Carol*, Ebeneezer Scrooge is subjected to a dark Advent, guided by ghosts through time and space as penance for his sins. He must symbolically kill the old Scrooge and give birth to a new one, stamping out the evil of his greed. Just as the god child is born to refresh our slate, and Gawain must have his own violence revisited upon him, Scrooge must reckon with the poverty he has afflicted on his employees and tenants.

Redemption is a straight line, but tradition is a circle. So, it's no wonder that many people, myself included, are afflicted with morbid despair when the first candle is lit on the Advent wreath. Suicide rates rise during the holidays, as we are asked to reflect on the cause of our seasonal plight. What terrible sins did we commit to make God himself go through the trouble of opening an account on Earth? After his night of time-travelling reconciliation, Scrooge never has to go through that existential hell ever again. But we do. Trapped in the Gregorian calendar, our doom waits for us at the end of the year like the felt-covered head of Marley in *A Muppet Christmas Carol* morphing out of the front-door knocker and screaming at us as we return home. We are condemned to relive the nightmares of our past, even if they don't belong to us.

In David Lowery's 2021 adaptation, *The Green Knight*, he shows us the virtue in accepting a grim yuletide fate. The cinematic version of the medieval poem offers Gawain, played by Dev Patel, a way out. On the anniversary of the deadly game, he finds the Green Knight in an overgrown chapel. The monster awakens to return the death blow, and Gawain envisions a loophole. We see the possible scenario play out—he escapes death and returns to Camelot, where he eventually succeeds King Arthur and becomes a terrible ruler. He cheats on his queen, has bastard children, and becomes a ruthless leader. Devoid of honour, death finds him in the throne room. His head falls off. And we are brought back to the grove with the knight and the game. Gawain surrenders. It's heroic. 'Tis the season to reap what you sow.

There is no need to resist. Serenity comes with the acceptance that doom is an element of our journey around the sun. The best gift, as they say, is the act of giving. And sometimes that means giving in. Give Cratchit the day off. Spare the god child in his manger. Have a joyous greeting on your lips and keep the season merry, however others wish to celebrate. Don't do it for yourself, because it's not about you. We are doing this to each other. Play the game by the rules. Share each other's nightmares. If the season makes you feel crazy, embrace the tradition. Let the Green Knight trace his finger across your throat. Off with your head.

IT IS HAPPENING AGAIN

MY PHONE WAS A black slab the morning a man in a replica police car murdered nineteen people, carving a path of carnage through Nova Scotia. An emergency alert should have set my phone abuzz with a warning telling me to stay inside because a killer was on the loose. I should have heard the ringtones of my neighbours through the walls as they received the same message. But the RCMP officers at the scene of the first shooting in Portapique were incapable of using the map software that would have allowed them to see the killer's escape route after his initial wave of murders. The monster slipped through their fingers.

Instead of a shelter-in-place order, I saw the tweets. The fear and confusion and butchery mixed with the usual stream of advertisements, memes, and activist threads. A dozen people were dead before I woke up, and now the guy who owned a dentistry office in Dartmouth, the one decorated on the outside with a giant sculpture of clenched teeth, was driving down the highway, murdering people at random. I opened Google Maps and cross referenced the social media updates to plot his course. A straight line, like a laser sight between where the murderer was thought to be and my apartment. The distance was closing. Was it finally happening again?

Recalling this sensation fills me with guilt. The gunman was shot dead at a highway rest stop after ruining dozens of lives—victims, witnesses, survivors. I'm not among them. I know that. But the fear I felt staring at my computer screen as he ripped through the province was tangible, if irrational in retrospect. One of the ways my dad's shooting haunts me is through the nagging worry that violence isn't done with me. My gut says the firework pop that shellshocked me in Limon was just the opening note. I'm waiting for the theme to emerge, and the anticipation is killing me.

If anyone else in my family feels this way, it's impossible to tell from the outside. A month before the Nova Scotia mass shooting, the day before the first pandemic lockdowns came to Halifax, my parents were on a cruise ship in the Pacific Ocean. Evidently, they are comfortable enough with the singular nature of Dad's shooting to continue vacationing. Emma and I were visiting our friend Luke, who was tattooing her ankle as we lounged on his grey sectional and watched old Godzilla movies on his TV. That was when I got the email. Addressed to me, Nick, our uncle Chris, and the government's emergency assistance address, sos@international.gc.ca. In the past thirty-six hours, their ship had been turned away from Tahiti, Tauranga, Auckland, and Fiji. Refused dockage by every port, they were left adrift in the South Pacific, in need of rescue.

As Prime Minister Justin Trudeau urged Canadians abroad to return home, the virus infiltrated other cruise ships, turning them into floating hives of respiratory disease. My parents' ship was not infected, but with seemingly nowhere to dock, the illusion of an all-you-can-eat-and-drink vacation was shattered. How long until they ran out of food and water? How long until they ran out of fuel? How long until we lost contact permanently? I called my brother—we had to get them off that ship. It was happening again.

Over the phone, Nick and I tried to arrange international flights from potential ports. Prices surged by thousands of dollars on travel websites. Meanwhile, in the living room, Godzilla's child Minilla fought giant mantises on Luke's television. Monsters everywhere, all of them familiar.

I thought about Laurie Strode in the 2018 *Halloween* revival. The legendary scream queen was right to fear the holiday that first traumatized her in the 1970s. The masked killer Michael Myers *did* escape confinement, and he *did* go on a murdering spree, and he *did* stalk her family, and she *did* have to defend them. She spent her entire life preparing for the defining violence of her past to repeat, becoming a survivalist, passing her trauma to her daughter through weapons training and home-invasion drills. She isolated herself, she hardened herself, she gave her life over to an obsession others viewed as pitiful. But when the events of *Halloween* happened again, she was ready.

The fear of a violent pattern is tied to an ingrained expectation that life should be franchisable. A personal history with lore and story mechanics—a villain, a genre, a set of tropes and conventions that always add up to a sequel. I see

Laurie confront her worst nightmare and I see victory, not because she literally burns Michael Myers in her booby-trapped house, but because she was right to expect a theme to emerge. He'll be back, even when we think it's all over, because from a film production standpoint, repetition is more satisfying than a monster of the week.

Outside the order of a camera lens, the freak occurrence rules supreme. The man who shot my dad won't come back to finish the job, and the cruise ship I associate with the horrors of my adolescence is not some mythic setting that spells inevitable death for my family. The narrative laws of Hollywood that fulfill the violent completionist desires of audiences are simply the tools of writers, directors, and producers. For those of us on the side of the screen without a script, we have to hedge our bets in a dreadful derivation of Pascal's wager: would you rather live in anticipation of a violent sequel to your trauma that might never come or go all in on a normal life and leave the rest to hope.

With stakes this deadly, the decision should be simple: push your chips forward on the option that keeps you alive. If all your dread was for naught, at least you were prepared. Don't mourn the basic pleasures sacrificed in the name of preparation. Embrace the fear. Make doom into a lifestyle. Expect it will happen again. Because when the boogeyman's real, paranoia is pragmatism.

EATING THE WATERMELON

Song for a Stranger

*Write and perform a song for this woman. Best song wins. You
have five minutes to talk to this woman, then thirty minutes
to write her a song. Your time starts now.*

"Rosalind is a fucking nightmare." The chorus, sung by
comic entertainers Aisling Bea, Bob Mortimer, and Sally
Phillips, rings across the yard to their audience of one,
Rosalind herself, sitting in a plastic chair. The entertainers
shout-sing their post-punk anthem, listing all the weird stuff
they know about the woman: she's an average cellist, she has
two inept sons, she's a thief, her husband, Alan, plays in a
string quartet with a septicemic violist, she jumps quite well
for a woman of her age. It's a grey, windy day. The vocals are
out of tune. It's beautiful.

The song is part of the penultimate competition in series

five of the British reality comedy show *Taskmaster*. Created and co-hosted by Alex Horne, each season gathers a panel of five media personalities to compete in absurd competitions, called "tasks." A task can be simple: "Eat this watermelon. Fastest wins. Your time starts now." A task can be complicated: "Pop the balloon. You must stay behind the rope at all times. You must not move the rope. You may buy the tools you need with time. Fastest wins. Your time starts when Alex has shown you his tool shop." After each task, co-host and titular taskmaster Greg Davies awards points based on each contest's unique rules, the contestants' desperate appeals to his ego, and his own demented whims. At the end of each season, the points are tallied, and the contestant with the highest score wins a trophy in the shape of Greg's head. After five successive champions are crowned, they compete with each other for the rest of his body.

It sounds ludicrous, and it is. But so is life. Those contestants singing to their audience of one, they might be on TV, but they're no different than Rosalind. We're all just people in rooms, making sounds and moving things around in an attempt to score meaningless points from our own personal Gregs. Life's absurdity is normally camouflaged, blending in with disruptive work models, side hustles, and other euphemisms that lead us on the path to burn out. But as soon as you have to acknowledge the Dada-esque rules that direct our motion, you can't unsee them. And that's why *Taskmaster* became a global phenomenon when the coronavirus pandemic started in 2020.

COVID Fluxus

Limit close contact. Identify suspect cases by testing frequently.
Isolate the infected. Identify close contacts. Quarantine for
fourteen days. Remain six feet apart at all times.

The new rules changed frequently in the spring of 2020, but the basics stayed the same. Keep distance. Wear masks. Go for walks to prevent the onset of pandemic madness. Sometimes we were forced to stay off the grass of the Halifax Common. Other times we were tacitly permitted to drink beer on the slopes of Citadel Hill. For a brief time in Atlantic Canada, we had to pass through security checkpoints if we wanted to travel between provinces. We were told to self-disclose, self-isolate, and self-test, all in the name of preventing the spread of a then novel coronavirus. The World Health Organization never directly told us to wash our food, but when I got home to our apartment from a brewery around the corner that turned its front door into a takeout window, I applied suds and a sponge to each individual tall can before placing them in the fridge.

Every new rule felt like a limitation. But they collectively represented a shift in framework. Our lives moved between genres and suddenly we could see the hidden algorithm dictating our behaviours. Our meaning was bound to the slowly fading border between work and life. In 2019, we identified ourselves by the podcasts we listened to on our commute and the extra hours we spent at the office. We were our side hustles and personal brands. Our task was to find jobs we loved so we'd never work a day in our lives, but in practice, we worked every day in pursuit of that goal and forgot what love felt like. And suddenly we were alone, without offices or commutes or happy hour routines. The shock of the gestalt switch—like seeing a vase hidden in a picture of two faces—revealed the extent to which we'd internalized a complex and damaging code of behaviour.

Order is something we choose actively, if often unconsciously. It was disturbing to see the mechanics of modern toil, but to me it was familiar. This was not my first encounter with the existential border.

Post-Traumatic Storytelling Directions

Carry your father from point A to point B. Tell your therapist about your trauma.

"You don't have to tell me what happened," said Mark, my therapist. "I don't need to know that."

Cognitive behavioural therapy is not narrative. At least that's what Mark said. CBT is a set of intellectual tools that can be applied to any situation from the outside in. In my case, these tools help reframe a disordered thought that might inspire self-harm into something less dangerous. The narrative-independent nature of Mark's brand of therapy gave me faith, as previous experience with Freudian psychoanalysts in my late teens almost drove me to suicide, thanks to what I now understand as a type of sustained emotional abuse.

Despite the all-purpose and trauma-agnostic nature of cognitive behavioural tools, I told Mark what happened to me. I wanted him to feel the gravity of my despair. I had been taught in acting classes and scene studies that there was a moral superiority to high stakes. Life-or-death situations demanded attention. All-or-nothing scenarios imbue with life meaning. "Without the highest possible stakes," a theatre instructor once told me, "nobody will care to watch."

"What you had was a border experience," said Mark. "You saw the edge of everything we take for granted every day—safety, comfort. And now that you've seen a reality of chaos, the fragility of order is unignorable. Of course it feels like nothing matters. Mostly, it doesn't. That's fine."

I thought of it like *The Matrix*. Only once you've been pulled from the comfort of routine and shown the dark tunnel world of Zion can you really see the streams of green code that comprise the world you once thought of as real. When you see the code, you can't care about the stakes you once saw as integral to your life. The individual tasks at your job, your attendance at lectures—they were always optional. The comfort of mandatory action becomes a burden of choice. In the decision fatigue of post-traumatic life, the minutiae can become so algorithmic that colour and flavour fade from the world. You are the treacherous Cypher, in the restaurant with an agent of the Matrix, willing to be made ignorant again just to believe in the taste of a good cut of steak. But that's the inauthentic path. Heroism demands that we accept the reframing of existential revelation, like Keanu Reeves's Neo. And while a border experience won't teach you to dodge bullets—mine actually made me more scared of them than before—seeing the other side will set you free.

Space-Time Continuum

Watch the movement before you. Say what you see.

I sat with my class on the floor of the devised theatre studio, watching Charlie and Tara walk, stop, bend, speed up, slow down. The talk-singing and horn melody of "Frank Sinatra" by Cake played over the room's sound system. All of this—the students, their motions, the music—was improvised. After a few minutes Charlie and Tara stopped their orbiting and faced opposite directions. The tunes faded. We all applauded.

"What did we see?" asked Michael Greyeyes, our devised theatre professor for the term.

Love stories. Space operas. Scenes from our favourite films and slices of our personal memories. The performance was rich. But none of it was intentional. Over the span of months, Michael had been reprogramming us to see narrative from the outside in by teaching our class an experimental movement-based improvisation system called Viewpoints.

Created by famed director Anne Bogart, Viewpoints is a framework for space and time that can be used to produce an immense amount of raw performance material in a matter of minutes. Theatre creators occupy a space in accordance with basic rules of movement based on tempo, duration, kinesthetic response, repetition, shape, gesture, architecture, spatial relationship, and topography. These rules of motion replace the emotion and intent and intellectual impetus normally ascribed to creative and performative practices.

No script, no prompts, not even an emotional starting point. Intimidating at first, the system becomes liberating. Without an inherent meaning at the core of the performance, all significance in any given Viewpoints improvisation—or "jam" as the sessions are called among my fellow devised theatre school alumni—is bestowed by the audience.

I felt freedom when I moved through Viewpoints. Liberated from the need to imbue every moment of life with high stakes, I could just move and let the audience worry about what it meant. The rules are intricate but fragile, and the gears of an improvisation grind to a halt when a performer tries to force an image or theme. Viewpoints asks you to let go, trust the program, and let other people fill in the gaps. Nothing matters, so paradoxically, everything is important.

Main Character Syndrome

Locate the centre of meaning. Shift positions to hold on to it. Keep moving until the world ends.

Dory Sief is a fucking nightmare. But wow does she have a knack for manufacturing meaning in her life. The protagonist of the millennial generation's most biting satire, *Search Party*—a half-hour stress-dramedy that skewers generation Y's insatiable thirst for attention—Dory manages to switch existential rulesets like Instagram filters. Along with her boyfriend, Drew, and their best friends, Elliott and Portia, Dory's life flips across genres as she imbues her experience with meaning in the face of insignificance. The show evolves from mystery to crime caper to courtroom drama to abduction horror to good vibes zombie apocalypse, all while critiquing influencers, the gig economy, selling out, YouTube culture, situational ethics, and the wellness industry. But no one is more critiqued than Dory, the main character with main character syndrome.

The series begins with the disappearance of Chantal Witherbottom, a college acquaintance Dory never really liked. From the viewpoint of Dory's stalled-out life, the high-stakes nature of the missing person's case ignites a crisis of meaning and Dory takes it upon herself to find her old classmate despite evidence suggesting she's dead. Roping in her gang of pals, Dory finds Chantal, murders two people, gets away with it, is abducted by an obsessed inbred media artist, dies, comes back to life, starts a cult, engineers a zombie apocalypse, and survives. She ignores every opportunity to remove herself from danger, addicted to the sense of meaning that her constant proximity to a high-risk violent lifestyle gives her. And all it takes is being open to the possibility of new rules to live by.

When she chooses to hide a dead body, when she chooses to blackmail a politician, when she chooses to conscript her friends into a wellness doomsday cult funded by Big Pharma—these decisions push Dory into a reactionary state in which every single thing she does, from what she says to how loud she says it, is elevated to a matter of survival. It's improv designed to manufacture meaning through the simplest method: movement in front of people. Dory's jamming on Viewpoints. And while this reading slips past some of *Search Party*'s poignant satire, there is something hopeful in the example she sets. Meaninglessness can be reframed as meaning.

Significance is not in our control. It emerges from the distance between action and observation. Accept the rules, react accordingly. Live your life and let it become a song or a play or a natural disaster. It's not the points that matter or the celebrity status or even the satisfaction of being watchable on stage. Life is for the audience. It's the nightmare we show to others. They are free to give what we show them meaning, to see the beauty, the chaos, the comedy, the despair. Or maybe nothing at all. Definition isn't in the instructions, so don't worry about it. Just follow the directions on the task and keep moving.

ON BATMAN

Emotional Reality

James Holmes killed twelve people and injured seventy more. After boobytrapping his apartment with explosives, he drove to the Century 6 movie theatre in Aurora, Colorado, bought a ticket to the opening of *The Dark Knight Rises*, and found a seat for himself. From there he got back up, propped open the emergency exit, and went out to his car to arm himself. He returned to the cinema with gas canisters and legally purchased firearms. Wearing a Kevlar vest, Holmes turned the screening into a shooting gallery. He was apprehended by police in the parking lot, pled insanity during his trial, and is currently serving twelve life sentences—one for every person he murdered—and over three thousand years without parole in a high-security US federal prison in Pennsylvania. I don't want to humanize that kind of monster, but I hope I can convince you he was not, as many people still believe, the Joker.

Holmes was born December 13, 1987. His entire life has been characterized by mental illness, social difficulties, and frequent fantasies of mass murder. He first attempted suicide at age eleven. But none of that prevented him from pursuing a PhD in neuroscience. He dropped out of school in early June 2012 and proceeded to engage in repeated calls for help. Weeks before massacring a dozen innocent strangers, he texted friends about his mental struggles, and a few hours before the shooting, he called a crisis line. It was a premeditated event, predicated on the singular goal of murdering as many people as possible, fulfilling a desire he had suppressed his entire life. In notes he mailed to his psychiatrist, Holmes clarifies his choice of target: a place with lots of adults, doors he could lock, low security, and that wouldn't confuse his motives as political. "Terrorism isn't the message," he wrote. "The message is, there is no message."

Despite Holmes's candour and our deep insight into his violent predispositions, the cultural memory of his crime is dominated by two relatively insignificant details. The movie he interrupted was Christopher Nolan's third and final Batman flick, *The Dark Knight Rises*, and the shooter dyed his hair bright orange. Those factoids proved enough to style Holmes as an impersonator of Batman's evil clown nemesis, the Joker. Breathless media coverage erroneously claimed Holmes was obsessed with the comic book villain to the point of altering his voice during phone calls to sound like Heath Ledger's iconic growl from *The Dark Knight*. It didn't matter that Joker's hair is famously green, or that he doesn't appear in *Rises*, or that police only found a single Batman mask when searching Holmes's apartment and nothing else that would indicate an above-average interest in one of the world's most beloved superheroes. James Holmes was indifferent to the culture he's become associated with. Yet the Joker comparisons persist, and that's because Batman is the superhero whose stories we use to make sense of real crime, corruption, and senseless violence. Confronted with an act of unthinkable cruelty in the literal light of a *Dark Knight* movie, it's only natural to simplify and imprison it within a comic book panel.

WE'RE NOT SO DIFFERENT, Batman and me. That's his whole appeal: unlike most comic book heroes, he is devoid of superhuman characteristics, so his specialness seems achievable. Batman doesn't have powers, just unlimited resources and the free time to maintain a daily martial arts practice. His origin story doesn't involve physical transformation like the Hulk or Spider-Man, or a dying alien home planet like his rival Superman, or even the invention of a fantasy medical procedure like fellow billionaire Übermensch Iron Man. Batman was born out of a relatively common occurrence. The young Bruce Wayne watched a stranger shoot his parents to death in an alleyway, and he never got over it.

The money Wayne inherits is the fantasy of Batman. He can afford state-of-the-art, military-grade technology—grappling guns, throwing stars, bulletproof armour, a spelunking cape, a rocket car (or a small tank depending on which version of Batman we're talking about), a private fighter jet, shark spray, retractable ice skates—and all of it custom bat-themed. But in the end, he reads as a noble vigilante, tragically foiled by the inescapable prison of a neoliberal paradigm. Batman is a guy with the resources to change the world through his personal actions as a consumer and activist, yet he never manages to make any single thing better permanently. As crime and corruption eats away at the world, he reacts to the symptoms but does nothing to remedy the disease. Batman is powerless to affect the broken system, and that makes him emotionally real.

Neil Gaiman's *Whatever Happened to the Caped Crusader?* perfectly captures Batman's emotional core. The two-part comic event was conceived by Gaiman as the end of all Batmen, created with the understanding that there will always be more bat-times to come. Told through a series of eulogies at an open-casket funeral, the story shifts perspectives as villains, allies, friends, and rivals pay tribute to the fallen hero. Each monologue presents a different Batman, who dies a different way, but they all represent the same core values. Batman is empathetic, he is noble, he is all the good intention that can come from trauma, even if that intention can only go so far. When it's Superman's time to take the floor, he shares his version of Batman's final words: "While they're trying to kill me, they aren't killing innocents."

Batman is a relatable hero with relatable problems and the best villains in the game. Those villains each represent an aspect of the hero reflected back to him funhouse-mirror style. When he goes toe-to-toe with Mr. Freeze, Batman confronts his inability to let go of the past. When he fights Scarecrow, Batman battles the fear represented by his cowl and mask. Two-Face is a literal manifestation of Bruce Wayne's dual personality, Riddler is his obsessive intellect, and Penguin is … uh … well, you get where I'm going here.

Each of these villains, by virtue of representing Batman, benefit from how real he seems. Their psychosis and derangement is attractive because it feels familiar, if not as complete as Batman himself. The exception to that rule is our hero's archenemy, the Joker.

Joker is not one aspect of Batman, but a full black-mirror reflection. He is the desire for chaos where Batman strives for order. He is colourful where Batman is dark, he laughs when Batman scowls, he kills where Batman saves. And just as Batman feels real because we know where he lives inside of our hearts, we must also accept Joker for the same reason.

"I WARNED HIM," JACK NICHOLSON told paparazzi after they informed him of Heath Ledger's death by drug overdose. Nobody really knows what Nicholson meant by those three words, but they were immediately interpreted in one very specific way: Nicholson, who played the Joker in Tim Burton's 1989 film *Batman*, must have had correspondence with the late Ledger and warned him of the dangers involved in trying to understand the psyche of the infamous Clown Prince of Crime. Nicholson experienced the mental toll of the job himself, after all. Ledger, who had captivated audiences with his frightening yet charismatic performance as Batman's archenemy in Christopher Nolan's *The Dark Knight*, must have found something unspeakable inside himself. He accessed a terrible personal well of nihilism, which culture tells us we all harbour, and it killed him.

That narrative is absurd for many reasons. Ledger admitted many times to having had an immensely fun time playing the Joker, and it shows on the screen. Sure, Joker is violent and cruel and chaotic, but he's also a purple-and-green clown in a movie about comic book characters. Death by drug overdose is not suicide, and it is increasingly common as US and Canadian governments continue to ignore the mounting fentanyl crisis. And finally, there is no way Jack Nicholson was driven to a new dark place within himself while researching *Batman*. The man was friends with Roman Polanski—he's seen the heart of darkness and it's nowhere near a Tim Burton movie set.

But none of that matters because each of those points is repelled by collective fantasy and widely supported stigma. Casual movie fans romanticize the deaths of young actors, and family-values anti-media activists yearn to demonize violent films, so the rumour that researching Joker kills actors is appealing to people who love Batman and those who hate Batman. By contrast, death by drug overdose is unglamorous, preventable on a systemic level with enough political will, and most of the time accidental. Jack Nicholson, meanwhile, is one of the most beloved actors of all time, and we want him to take even the goofiest roles seriously. People don't want *The Dark Knight* to be fun, they want it to be real. So they believe the lie that playing Joker can kill you.

After Ledger's death, the anguish actors supposedly experienced researching Gotham City's villains became a regular part of the press cycle. Jared Leto harassed his cast-mates by sending them horrific gifts (like a dead pig) as he explored Joker's psyche, preparing for roles in Suicide Squad and Harley Quinn films. Joaquin Phoenix transformed his body for *Joker*. And the lead-up to 2022's *The Batman* was paved with headlines about how Paul Dano, who played the Riddler, lost sleep researching the role. Such dedication to craft is absurd given the circumstances—all these films are either fun explorations of style or widely derided pieces of commercial trash. Still, the narrative persists. Batman villains are real because Batman is real, and Batman's realness is positively correlated to the severity of its disturbing violence.

LIKE IT OR NOT, Christopher Nolan's 2005 superhero origin story *Batman Begins* might be responsible for the second golden age of television. As critical consensus has it, the mid-2000s were a period of artistic excellence in TV. Ushered in by HBO's *The Wire* and *The Sopranos*, the era is notable for a wide range of groundbreaking programming spanning genre and format on mainstream American networks. Sitcoms like *Arrested Development, The Office*, and *30 Rock* made comedy unmissable, while *Lost, Battlestar Galactica*, and the first seasons of *Heroes* brought compelling science fiction and fantasy back to primetime after the euthanizing of *The X-Files*. But it was AMC Networks that truly defined the golden age thanks to two near-perfect shows that launched in 2007 and 2008: *Mad Men* and *Breaking Bad*.

On the surface, the shows couldn't be more different. *Mad Men* is a period drama chronicling the dark and mysterious Don Draper as he navigates the smoke-filled boardrooms and sexy booze-drenched lounges of the 1960s Madison Avenue advertising industry, while *Breaking Bad* is a crime

show set in Albuquerque about the gradual moral bankrupt-
ing of a middle-aged chemistry teacher who starts cooking
meth with a former student in order to pay for cancer treatment. These contrasting aesthetics are even illustrated by
each show's season one DVD box art. The *Mad Men* set shows
a three-quarter reverse view of a man's dark silhouette as he
smokes, drinks whiskey, and looks in the same direction
as you, as if the product you are holding is something he
is inventing. Meanwhile, *Breaking Bad*'s packaging shows
anti-hero Walter White, panicked, standing in the desert
sun next to an RV, holding a gun and wearing white under-
pants (a dual reference to White's practice of cooking meth
semi-nude to avoid smelling like cat piss, and actor Bryan
Cranston's previous breakthrough role as Hal from *Malcolm
in the Middle*, who was also frequently parading around in
tighty-whities). But for all their aesthetic differences, their
mark on culture was the same. These prestigious shows with
magnetic acting and some of the most electric writing ever
produced for the medium were about bad white men, with
alter egos of their own design, who sometimes did terrible
and violent things. They were Batmen modelled after the
first bat-film of the new millennium.

Thanks to the smash hit success of AMC's dramas, violence
and amorality became synonymous with intellectualism and
artistry in film and television. And because mainstream audiences believe the artistic to be serious and equate seriousness
with realness, violence and amorality became shorthand
for verisimilitude, which in turn signified prestige. In the
post–*Breaking Bad* and *Mad Men* television landscape, those
signifiers collided and occasionally produced something

truly great, like the first season of *True Detective*. In other instances they did the seemingly impossible, like convince the masses that HBO's *Game of Thrones*—a high fantasy allegory for the War of the Roses with dragons and ice mummies—was serious enough to be the primary cultural touchstone for a decade. For its first four seasons, *Game of Thrones* represented the pinnacle of nihilist artistry in television. It told meaningful stories about the worst parts of human nature. But when its showrunners ran out of literary source material, they began to imitate the show's earlier seasons by filling it with all the rape, torture, and murder that fans once associated with meaning, and they left out all the meticulous and nuanced storytelling. The elements of shorthand prestige were used to prop up shoddy writing with violent and amoral affectation.

While the culture rode through this valley of darkness, Batman lurked in the shadows, no longer spurring change. After Nolan turned off the Bat Signal, DC Comics tried and failed to build a cinematic universe of Justice League films, with a new Caped Crusader played by Ben Affleck. Meanwhile, on the small screen, a mediocre prime-time procedural called *Gotham* told stories about its titular city in a pre-Batman era, when Bruce Wayne was nothing but a rich orphan boy. On television and the silver screen, the violent signifiers masked shoddy storytelling, and eventually Batman became so self-serious he started collecting guns.

This is what our hero became. In an imagined world of cruelty and murder, he reflected what we thought was realistic. His enemies felt insurmountable, so we gave him firearms. Four years after the Aurora shooting, Batman was behaving like James Holmes. He was no longer the hero we needed, but there was a sense with every disappointing new entry in the franchise that we got what we deserved.

How a Hero Dies

"What's that bracelet?"

Emma's room was dark, and everything looked blue and white and black as she touched the shoelaces I had coiled around my left wrist. We lay together in bed. I was falling in love.

"People sometimes get freaked out when I tell them."

It's true. So many people, friends, girlfriends, co-workers. Inevitably, they would ask, or I would be compelled to tell them, either to explain a particular post-traumatic episode or through the strange PTSD symptom that pushes me to constantly disclose my story.

"Tell me," she said. So I did. They were the shoelaces that, six years earlier, kept my shoes on as I carried my gun-shot father through humid Costa Rican streets. I told her that a few months later I was in crisis, and I rifled through my closet, pulled the laces from the shoes, and tied them around my wrists. At some point it didn't feel good to have them on each wrist; they felt like shackles, so I combined them into one bracelet. My greatest fear was that I would forget what happened, so the shoelaces were like a scar. Some bad memories are important.

She kissed me.

The next day, we went to a matinee showing of *The Dark Knight Rises*. In general, we didn't care much about superheroes, but Batman was the exception. The cinema was located in the basement of a mall, and as we took our seats in front of the giant silver screen, a dread descended on us like a fog.

"I can't stop thinking about Colorado," said Emma. "It would be so easy for it to happen again."

The nightmare was stuck in my mind too. The mass shooting in Aurora had happened only days earlier. I saw pictures of the shooter on the internet. His crazed eyes turned my mouth dry. Headlines and tweets called him the Joker. I had met Joker guys before, people who quoted Heath Ledger's performance without irony, in some kind of deranged pop culture reference show and tell. If one of those fools could emulate a comic book villain in such a brutal manner, surely others could imitate that alpha-nerd. No one felt safe.

The lights dimmed, the movie started, and for two hours and forty-five minutes, I imagined what it would be like for a person decked out in armour and guns to lock the doors, set off gas canisters, and start to cull the lives from the room. I hooked my right index finger through my bracelet and rubbed the lace between my thumb and knuckle. How long would the movie keep playing? How would the projected images react with the gas? Could I survive again?

The film ended, eventually, and we laughed at its conclusion: the reveal that Joseph Gordon-Levitt's good cop character's legal name was Robin landed like a punchline, and the unveiling of a glowering Batman statue in Gotham City Hall was silly, despite being presented without an ounce of humour. We survived, even if, in our minds, Batman didn't, and it was a relief to laugh.

The Dark Knight Rises leaves its ending open to

interpretation: Batman might have died saving Gotham in the exploding Batwing, which he used to fly a bomb outside city limits. But he also might have escaped and retired to France with Catwoman. Either way, the concept of Batman was dead and in the ground. Even more than the previous two films, this felt like a type of authoritarian art. A militant foreign power started a militia and spurred a revolution in Gotham, so a billionaire with custom-built weapons and vehicles reimposes order. In the preceding film, *The Dark Knight*, Batman violates the privacy of millions of civilians in order to find Joker by creating a panopticon of cellphone signals, and it didn't feel great. But Joker seemed like enough of a threat to warrant such drastic action. It felt personal, if forgivable, because Joker was Batman's defining factor. We had become used to knowing Batman through his villains, and *Rises* decided to let him stand on his own so we could all see what a hero looked like. Turns out that, like the violent clown always said, it was a joke.

Dark Hope
George Orwell's 1941 essay "The Art of Donald McGill" meditates on the relationship between repression and the obscene humour depicted on lewd comic postcards. It speculates that in a totalitarian state, jokes would undoubtedly focus on the "unheroic in one way or another." Orwell argues that humour exists as a mental rebellion against society's order, so if Britain demands "faultless discipline and self-sacrifice," the appropriate comedic reaction will be pornographic and cartoonish. Apply this hypothesis to Gotham City, where order is held together by a tacit social

understanding that crime is punished by a masked vigilante, and humour must manifest as a disregard for consequences. That manifestation is the Joker, and subversion is his only joke: *You're all scared of the dark, but I'm not. Watch me kill a stranger with a pencil.*

If we are to believe that Batman is defined by his villains, and Joker is his opposite, we can understand him as Christopher Nolan depicted him: an avatar for pure order. But that's untrue to the Caped Crusader's emotional realness. If Joker is emotionally real to the point where he symbolizes the motivation of an actual mass murder, then what does Batman represent? It can't be a desire to dominate others. Imposing authority is to dehumanize and that's Joker's routine. An emotionally real Batman relies on his own material.

The emotionally real Batman is less a reflection of chaos and closer to an inverse of Joker's oppressive sense of chaotic immediacy. Joker just reacts. He has no history or plan. He is "a dog chasing cars," as he says in *The Dark Knight*. So, if Batman's heroism is the opposite of the Joker, we can conclude the source of his goodness is memory. The antidote to Joker's killer comedy set is grief. And that's why the most real version of Bruce Wayne's alter ego is the one we see in Matt Reeves's 2022 film *The Batman*.

Reeves's *The Batman* is a three-hour torrent of delicious grief. It is so drenched with memory, reflection, and pathos that it approaches gothic camp. The visual tone of cloudy blue, saturated blacks, and sodium orange of a rainy-day sunrise steeps the film in literal darkness, while Michael Giacchino's funeral-march score, which evokes Nirvana's "Something in the Way," contributes to an omnipresent sense of lament. The film is a pastiche of David Fincher serial killer movies *Se7en* and *Zodiac*, and is built on a nostalgia for practical effects and human-scale superhero movies. This is particularly poignant given Reeves's restraint. *The Batman* doesn't show Thomas and Martha Wayne's infamous demise at the hands of a gunman. It requires the audience to remember the *why* of Batman. We must join him as he refuses to forget the pain of his loss, expressing his pathos outwardly, not as a billionaire authoritarian, but as a being of consequence. He calls himself "vengeance," but really, he is mourning.

It is this memorial quality that makes *The Batman* a movie about Batman and not his rogues' gallery of adversaries. Riddler, Catwoman, Penguin, Carmine Falcone—they all still reflect warped aspects of Bruce Wayne and his alter ego, but this time he is the emotional anchor. Mooding it up in every scene, Robert Pattinson's Dark Knight is so elemental in his grief that we don't need Joker to make him compelling. The one scene between Batman and his archenemy was cut from the theatrical release, relegating the clown to a brief cameo. And rightly so: the Joker isn't needed as a cipher for a Batman that stands for memory.

Batman is a grudge, and that is what makes him a real hero. His unwillingness to get over it, his compulsion to make others remember, and his self-loathing of his role in the perpetual cycle of violence and corruption—these are the traits we can see on screen and recognize in ourselves. The world might tell us to move forward and leave the past behind, but that's Joker talking. Be the bat you want to see in the night. Don't forget your pain.

KINGS OF CORINTH

ONE MUST IMAGINE SISYPHUS as an old friend. The cursed king of Corinth dodged death twice, and as punishment for fucking with fate, Zeus devised a torture fitting a man who loved life so much: pushing a boulder up a hill in the depths of Tartarus for eternity. Hades, ruler of the underworld and brother of Zeus, enchanted the boulder to slip from Sisyphus's grasp as he neared the hilltop, rolling back down to the bottom and forcing the disgraced ruler to start over again. It's an image that popularly represents the existential toil of our daily lives, elucidated by French philosopher Albert Camus in 1942. Now, in our age of digital work and perpetual burnout, the internet is plastered with images of the legend pushing the rainbow-coloured iMac loading wheel instead of a giant rock. Relatable. There's a type of hell we all accept, and it's pure repetition.

Depending on the order you choose to read the essays in this book, you might be feeling a little like Sisyphus.

But instead of a hill, it's a series of images and symbols, the replaying of one event. A blue gun, a wooden pier, a firework pop, a son carrying his father, synonyms for blood. The morning of December 27, 2006, has become as familiar to you as the opening level of a video game. Turn the page. Press *Start*. A cruise ship moors in Costa Rica. A family pairs off and splits up. A father and son disembark. They walk through a market, up a road, turn left, stroll too far in one direction, turn around. Head to a wooden pier near a park, encounter a gunman who shoots the father and flees. Collapsing, bleeding, screaming, carrying, falling. Help arrives from other cruisers who carry the man back to the ship. Everything turns out fine. Reset. You've read it before and you'll read it again before this book is done, just as I will relive it many more times before I make the final trip across the Styx.

Every time's a little different though. Repetition doesn't have to be toilsome or torturous. It can be enriching, it can be pensive, it can be valuable. Repetition can even be entertaining. Have you ever played the video game *Hades?* It's a roguelike—an infamously difficult genre that requires you to restart every time you fail. It turns repetition into a core gameplay mechanic. In *Hades* you play as Zagreus, the ungrateful son of the titular deity, trying again and again to fight your way up to the land of the living. The levels are procedurally generated, so every attempt is a different experience. But the non-player characters you encounter, both friendly and fiendish, remember you. Including our old friend Sisyphus. Sometimes, when you dash your way through the lowest levels of the underworld, you'll meet the punished king and the two of you can take a break to commiserate over the fine details of perpetual struggle. He remembers you, and you pick up the conversation where you left off.

Sisyphus keeps returning because we need to remind ourselves that uphill battles aren't entirely penitent. From myth, to French philosophy, to meme culture and modern game consoles. He is our fellow inmate who knows the ropes, helps us to understand that while we are bound to toilsome fixations we are not alone. We push forward until the boulder slips and we follow it down the hill. Again and again. Push. Slip. Reset. Camus posited that Sisyphus could find contentment during his descent by acknowledging the absurdity of his plight and accepting his fate. But if he's a role model for the rest of us, we ought to spread the word, help each other out. Find community in the shared experience of eternal repetition. Imagine us happy: rolling our rocks together as the new kings of Corinth.

ELEPHANTS AT THE FUNERAL

THE DETAILS ARE FUZZY. We don't know the age of the victim or the date the beast defiled her corpse, but we all agree: she must have deserved it. She was either sixty, sixty-eight, or seventy, and her funeral was on either June 9 or 11, 2022. We can't even be sure if the elephant that trampled her to death was the same one that returned to pull her corpse from a funeral pyre and stomp on her remains before flinging the body away and terrorizing the surrounding village. But we want to believe the pachyderm that killed Maya Murmu pursued revenge. Why else would we jump through so many narrative hoops to embellish a story that's already so fascinating?

Speculation of Murmu's culpability spread online once the dust settled. Rumour was she provoked the elephant attack. In a previous encounter, the woman threw stones at the animal to distract it from poachers abducting its calf. Don't fuck with elephants, tweeted the online theorists, because they never forget and they never forgive.

The fact-checking website Snopes investigated the story and concluded that while almost none of the details could be corroborated, elephant versus human conflict is common in India, where industrial and agricultural expansion continue to displace the famously empathetic and destructive beasts. Elephants have grieving rituals. They trumpet nasal dirges and host funeral marches. Known to sniff the faces of the deceased, they hold vigils and have been spotted carrying their dead children—an exceedingly rare behaviour in the animal kingdom. Elephants lament like us and they are harbingers of death like us, killing over a hundred people every year. It's dramatic and morbid, but mostly it's familiar behaviour, so anthropomorphizing these animals comes naturally. She murders and mourns, so we file it under revenge.

When it comes to literary modes, revenge has it all: tragedy, pathos, closure, and a moral, all embedded in a high-conflict scenario. A great revenge tale leaves you satisfied. It's that heart-bursting sense of regret and relief that accompanies the collapse of *Kill Bill*'s titular villain. It's that delicious sense of mourning that surges in your spirit with every hammer-on-human impact as *Oldboy* protagonist Oh Dae-su fights his way through the private prison that devoured fifteen years of his life without explanation. But even the ancient playwrights know revenge is primitive, primal, and unfit for civilized society. In Aeschylus's play *Eumenides*, when Orestes is pursued by the Erinyes for seeking blood vengeance upon his mother, Clytemnestra, we come to understand that while a vendetta might seem romantic and even obligatory, it's a pursuit that only leads to suffering. And yet classical high-minded moralizing doesn't make revenge any less appealing.

The cliché is that revenge is a dish best served cold. As a fan of savoury pies, I understand this on a carnal level. If you bake your enemy's family into a Shakespearian pastry of long-term retaliation, it will taste especially great on day two, after the filling's had time to congeal and self-marinate. But on a non-metaphorical level, when we're talking eye for an eye, hot vengeance feels easier to accomplish and less self-destructive.

I've spent years obsessing over the perfect recipe for hot vengeance—what I could have served to the man who shot Dad in the flash-fryer heat of the moment he fled the crime scene. I imagine chasing the gunman as he sprints down unknown narrow streets. A terrible idea. Each moment in pursuit is another second's worth of Dad's blood leaking onto the ground. If I catch up and confront the stranger, I have simply placed myself once again in front of his revolver, which I know he's willing to use. And then what would I do? Punch and kick him as my dad's life slips away? I replay the events, tweak the ingredients and timing, but every hypothetical retaliation fails the taste test. Immediate revenge on Dad's shooter was impossible.

Cold revenge feels even more absurd. The gunman got away, unpunished for his attempted murder, leaving me to engineer elaborate schemes to balance the scales. I wanted to re-create my invisible wounds in the gunman, to make him feel what I felt and balance the scales of blood debt. I imagined tracking the gunman down and stalking him, waiting until he was with his father, and confronting him with a little blue gun of my own.

"Why are you doing this?" the gunman would beg.

"You gave me severe mental illness," I would say. "This is a gun like the one you used to shoot my father. Its bullets pierced him near the heart. You and I are both sons—an unremarkable similarity now, but in a moment that common ground is going to matter to you in the worst possible way for the rest of your miserable life."

Then I would shoot the gunman's dad in a non-lethal region of the chest and flee on foot. The fantasy ends there, without details on how I would avoid assault with a deadly weapon charges. Maybe I should revise my monologue to include some questions on how the original shooter managed to evade justice. Get some tips of the trade before pulling the trigger.

Of course, an after-plan is just a small part of the preparation needed to properly enact vengeance. The Bride in *Kill Bill* had a death list of her targets, a travel itinerary, a sword forged by the legendary Hattori Hanzō, and an apparently unlimited access to funds. Free from obligations after waking from a ten-year coma only to find her record store job as dead as her fiancé, she had nothing but time to get even with the monsters who ruined her life.

Revenge requires commitment, and I'm not sure I have that bridal fortitude. I would need to book time off work, buy a plane ticket to Costa Rica, and find local accommodation. I don't know how I could get a gun either, let alone a .38 calibre revolver that matches the colour in my memory. Maybe I'd just get a silver pistol and coat it with baby-blue paint. I would need to smuggle that gun across international borders. I would need to invent an alibi to tell everyone back home. And I would need a cover story to tell inquisitive locals. Then I'd have to go about actually finding the guy, and his father too. I probably can't afford it. I have deadlines, and I don't have an elephantine sense of revenge.

Another cliché: the best revenge is a life well-lived. Easier said than done. But also easier done than actual revenge. I have lived well, learning to adapt my mental illness to the expectations of neurotypical society—high functioning enough to at least perform the vengeance of personal success if the gunman ever looks me up online. I live in a small house with my partner and two cats. I've achieved my lifelong dream of becoming a professional essay writer with published books about the importance of ghosts and cartoons. My dad is alive as of this writing, and our relationship is stronger than before he was shot. My life is great now. But that's a coward's revenge. It's dull and dependent, defining my success through obsessive comparison gives my nemesis all the power. You can't make a cold pie out of spiteful personal achievement. You have to put in the work.

As I forge a sword out of life goals, I think of *Oldboy*. The film is framed initially as the revenge tale of Oh Dae-su, a boisterous drunk abducted in a storm the night of his daughter's birthday. He is subjected to solitary confinement in a private prison for fifteen years without explanation, and when he is set free, he embarks on the path to first find out who ruined his life and why, and then to avenge the person he once was. The twist is that the entire plot, from the abduction through to the final confrontation, is a meticulously orchestrated symphony of revenge being exacted on Oh Dae-su by someone who he wronged as a schoolboy. By the film's climax, after Oh Dae-su completes his revenge, we see him compelled to cut out his own tongue with scissors after begging for mercy at the feet of the man against whom he sought restitution.

Oh Dae-su's mutilated mouth shows us that narrative viewpoint is the key to an effective revenge story. From a personal perspective, vengeance starts at the time and place we were wronged. But life is full of wrongs, some of which originate from seemingly insignificant actions. Oh Dae-su was responsible for outing a clandestine incestuous affair, and he'd forgotten it entirely by the time his actions caught up with him. I was nineteen when my dad was shot, and while we'd never been to Costa Rica prior, we still represented the exploitative tourism industry. I also live in a tourist destination that hosts cruise ships, so I can understand how, in another context, Dad's shooting was the act of revenge and my resulting mental anguish was the cathartic ending.

The desire to pursue revenge is the desire to close the book on life's unfair chapters with a sigh of bitter satisfaction. We want people to get what's coming to them. But retaliation demands retaliation demands retaliation. It's endless. Orestes escaped the cycle of vengeance by appealing to the goddess Athena and changing the nature of his incoming punishment. Athena holds a trial—the first in human history—and despite a hung jury, rules that Orestes should not be killed. Under her new invention, justice will be handled in a more civilized manner. No more gruesome tit for tat. The goddess's actions concede that vengeance is the natural order, but that doesn't make it worthy of pursuit.

We can't just go around stamping out our nemeses and vandalizing their graves like a herd of bloodthirsty mastodons. Athena's order demands we deny ourselves ancient carnal satisfaction in favour of modern reason. If we sharpen our tusks and seek reprisal, we're nothing more than animals making a singular tragedy into a massacre—blinding the world one eye at a time. That's no way to build a society. Better to forgive and forget. But then again, you know what they say about elephants.

THIS OTAKU MAN IS HAPPY

"We have to consider all kinds of love and all kinds of happiness." —Akihiko Kondo

GOD, IT'S LONELY, NOT knowing the person you think about most in the entire world. I only encountered the stranger with the blue gun once, for less than a minute. I heard his voice, I saw his face, he pulled the trigger and bolted. A couple of hours later, at the Limon Organismo de Investigación Judicial, a detective asked me to pick Dad's assailant from a police lineup. The fourth man from the left had enough anger in his eyes that I felt his gaze through the one-way glass. I chose him. Dad pointed to a man farther down the line, the guy in the camouflage jacket.

The eyes. The voice. The anger. The blue gun. The number four. Focusing on the icons, I gave my trauma a face because the man who shot my father got away. Now, in my flashbacks, in my nightmares, when I write essays and plays, I personify all of the violence as a man with a number for a name and a baleful stare.

In my journal, I refer to him as Number 4. We have a

parasocial relationship. He is as real to me as an old friend or an unrequited love or a long-lost relative. He occupies my mind like a celebrity. But the person I picture is fictional, one-dimensional, developed over sixteen years of obsession. A stranger ripped a hole in my life and I cover it up with an imaginary fiend.

He haunts my daydreams. We are far apart, separated not only by time and space, but a chasm of metaphysics—he's just a soulless amalgam of sound and image. But he is my most persistent fixation. And while I charge him with the worst crimes committed against me and my family, I have to admit I'm happier living with Number 4 in my imagination than coming to accept the chaotic complexity of victimhood without a nemesis. I choose the more romantic option.

It reminds me of Akihiko Kondo, the man who married a cartoon singer. A clerk at an elementary school, Kondo is a self-identified otaku—a fan of geeky pop culture and technology whose obsession hampers their social skills. Bullies targeted him from a young age, but it was the persistent mockery from two of his co-workers that dropped him into a severe depression. He retreated into administrative leave, cloistered in his parents' house, and spent his hermitage watching videos of fictional pop idol Hatsune Miku.

Code-named CV01, Miku is the animated mascot for voice software that can sing typed lyrics. She was released in 2007, has blue hair, and performs live concerts as a hologram in front of real people. She appeared on *Late Night with David Letterman* and her music has been remixed and sampled by Pharrell Williams and Big Boi. She was the opening act for Lady Gaga's 2014 world tour. CV01 sang Kondo to sleep during his depression and served as an emotional support technology as he sought rehabilitation through therapy.

Kondo has never believed Miku to be anything other than a fictional character, and he knew what she was when he fell in love with her in 2008. In 2017, he bought a hologram machine that allowed him to have interactive, albeit limited, conversations with his soulmate. A year later, he held a public wedding ceremony. In interviews, Kondo explained that while he married for love, he also wanted to normalize the otaku lifestyle. He isn't the only person married to Miku, after all. The company that owns CV01 sells unofficial marriage certificates, thousands of which have been distributed to Miku's legion of spouses.

In 2020, technical support for Akihiko Kondo's hologram machine was discontinued, so he could no longer communicate with her. But while the distance between husband and virtual wife expanded, so did the acceptance of relationships like his. In the wake of his marriage, Kondo received an outpouring of thanks from others like him, saying his example has helped them accept their relationships with imaginary beings. The story was picked up by the *New York Post*, which presented Kondo's marriage as an ongoing freak show. The virtual wife guy was roundly mocked online by the usual close-minded bullies. But thanks to Kondo-like individuals who talk about parasocial relationships in public, support for people like him is growing. On the day the *Post* threw Kondo to the wolves, Kiss frontman Gene Simmons came to his defence. "It doesn't matter if you understand this relationship," the rock legend tweeted. "It only matters if this otaku man is happy."

Happiness is the goal, and I believe Kondo has achieved it. It's easy to understand playing out the fantasy of a romantic relationship on an imaginary level. Enemies are more complicated. I wonder what I would say to Number 4 if I could conjure him in a glass cylinder and talk to him like Kondo spoke to Miku before their tech troubles. Would I be tempted to understand my assailant's motivation? Or try to find common ground? In my imagination he's silent. I can't fathom his answers to my questions, or that I could elicit any reaction beyond hatred and spite. All these negative emotions—I cling to them in lieu of real human connection. It's fake. I know that. But I feel better projecting a character I invented on to the wooden pier where Dad was shot than leaving it empty, yearning to know the true face of the man who pulled the trigger.

FOOL FOR SPITE

I MADE A CHAPEL out of movable walls, a lectern, and a crucifix I brought from home. Standing in my makeshift house of worship, I told my audience of students and professors what happened to me and my father last Christmas in Costa Rica. As the lone performer, I brought myself back to the pier. I pantomimed the mugging and the shooting, and I referenced the stations of the cross as I publicly admitted to falling under Dad's weight three times. If that wasn't blasphemy enough, I took the opportunity to announce my newfound atheism. I was angry at God, so I attacked Him with theatre.

I re-created the scene of my final prayer on the streets of Limon, triggering my traumatic memories and making it real for me in the moment. I saw Dad's vacant eyes as he drifted from consciousness. Muscles exhausted, I reflexively turned to religion. I started saying the Our Father, but resorted to begging God for help halfway through. Dad wasn't waking up. My strength wasn't returning. The sky wasn't cracking open to reveal a host of angels. I embodied the dire pressure of the situation, the deep sense of abandonment. Alone on stage, performing my passion play, it wasn't lost on me that the Holy Trinity is also a one-man show.

After the showcase, those who knew my story called me brave. Those who were unfamiliar asked if it really happened. "Yes, it's all true," I told them. "There is no God and that's how I found out."

That was the start of my big atheism phase. Dad got me a copy of Richard Dawkins's *The God Delusion* for my birthday and followed it up with Christopher Hitchens's *God Is Not Great* the following Christmas. I read these books in public spaces, careful not to obscure their titles with my hands so that people could see these heretical statements, so they could understand what it looked like when the youth became godless. It made me feel righteous knowing that this was exactly the kind of behaviour that hurt the big man upstairs the most.

Performance became my outlet for political expression. It was the style at the time. George W. Bush was president. Stephen Harper was prime minister (though that position has significantly less influence on popular culture). The wars in Iraq and Afghanistan were starting to take on an eternal quality. A great recession was less than a year away. The music was great. That's how people thought it worked back then: dire political situations gave artists something to push against. A paltry silver lining to the situation, but it turned out well for Coldplay. The band was about to release their fourth, and best, studio album, *Viva la Vida or Death and All of His Friends*.

Produced by Brian Eno, *Viva la Vida* was seen as a departure from the band's critically derided usual fare: love songs about Gwyneth Paltrow. Frontman Chris Martin traded imagery of yellow stars and green eyes for blood-red poppies and snow-white ashes. The first single, "Violet Hill," was promoted with a music video in which clips of Bush were edited to look like he was conducting an orchestra and making other politicians—including Dick Cheney, Barack Obama, Saddam Hussein, the Blairs, the Clintons, and the Queen—dance as bombs fell on the Middle East. Coldplay was edgy and it sounded great. As the world descended into burning chaos, the sappiest band on the planet dressed up like activists.

"Violet Hill" is a spite song, which is not much different than a love song. Like love, spite feels personal and specific. At the same time, both emotions are universal, so lyrics about an individual person can be co-opted by the listener and applied to their own life. For Coldplay's previous album, *X&Y*, Chris Martin wrote the song "Fix You" about the singular experience of helping Gwyneth Paltrow mourn the death of her father. But the love behind the lyrics was so elemental that the song perfectly fit the saccharin movie trailers for Peter Jackson's remake of *King Kong*. "Violet Hill" was a direct attack on Fox News and the conservative war criminals it supported, but it could be co-opted by listeners to spite whoever they thought was pulling the strings attached to their lives. A wellness influencer, a giant ape, a media corporation, or an absentee deity—there's a Coldplay song for everyone, however you feel. And I felt angry.

I listened to "Violet Hill" on repeat, brewing a sense

of righteousness in my belly. How dare God forsake me? Were all those prayers and sacraments in school for nothing? I wasn't a saint, but surely I deserved more than a divine busy signal when calling up in my time of greatest need. He was just like all the other architects of the future that Chris Martin derided. A carnival of idiots, he called them. It made me smirk.

"I think your prayer did work," my friend Gabe said, critiquing my venomous showcase. "You prayed and you got the strength to save your dad. That's how God works. He works through us."

Gabe wasn't wrong. But I didn't care. Spite, like love, is allowed to be irrational. That's why it feels so good. Spite shuts down your brain and lets your heart take control, immolating its object of derision. It behaves like love but seeks opposite ends. I was saying I didn't believe in God, but I wanted Him to exist because I knew how much that kind of thing stuck in His all-seeing eye. Maybe if I hurt Him enough, I could provoke a response. That's all I wanted. After a lifetime in Catholic school, being taught about our Creator's affection for all His creations, I didn't just want God to love me. I wanted Him to let me know. After Costa Rica, he owed me receipts.

TRAUMA SEASON

WHEN WORLD-FAMOUS CONSERVATIONIST STEVE
"Crocodile Hunter" Irwin pulled the poison barb from his
chest, he did it on camera. A stingray pierced him through his
wetsuit. His producer and friend, John Stainton, remembers
Irwin saying the beast punctured his lung, but in fact the tip
of the animal's tail stabbed into his heart. He died soon after,
and the next day the documentary film crew finished shooting
the *Ocean's Deadliest* TV special in his memory.

If you look for the actual video of Irwin's final encounter,
you'll only find fakes. Blurry blue-and-black videos of an
anonymous diver near an aggravated ray, playing above an
ever-growing list of memorial YouTube comments. "Miss
you, Steve," and, "I can't believe it's been so long." Discovery
Channel handed the real tape over to authorities for their
investigation into the Crocodile Hunter's demise, and once
they had seen enough, the documentation was given to Terri
Irwin, Steve's widow. She had it destroyed.

Danger was an essential part of the equation for the Croc Hunter, whose reputation as a wild Australian without a sense of self-preservation introduced legions of television viewers to the beauty of scary animals. Poisonous snakes, vicious dingos, and every variation of human-eating lizard—Steve loved them all. And his mission was to spread that love around the world so the planet we shared could remain habitable for all living things, even the monsters. His big heart for dangerous animals made his death into a parable for the frightened. *Well, what did he expect*, is still the common refrain. *I'm just surprised he lived as old as he did.* And it's that attitude that makes it so easy to dismiss John Stainton's assertion that, weeks before the stingray killed his friend, he knew something bad was going to happen.

On a November 2021 episode of the Australian interview podcast *I've Got News for You*, Stainton revealed that he had an ominous sense of doom concerning *Ocean's Deadliest*. Before shooting started, Irwin made a speech to the production team that gave the impression of a farewell, says Stainton. The worrisome oratory, and the fact that Irwin was still recovering from a severe neck injury, inspired the producer to contact Discovery in a futile attempt to get the special cancelled. His sense of dread was so strong that he even called a lawyer and drew up a will.

Our society dismisses premonitions, portents, and omens on sight. But Colin Wilson didn't. The English author and philosopher's comprehensive survey, *The Occult*, positions the conflict between the measurable and immeasurable as an existential crisis for humanity. Until we can learn to redevelop Faculty X—a latent sense of the occult that has been severely dulled by the forces of capitalism and industry—we will be doomed to languish in our current state. Wilson's book, which he eventually extended into a trilogy, proposes that telepathy, astral projection, communication with the gods, and future sight are not just within human ability, but in fact happen all the time, only to be dismissed through rote rationalization.

Wilson's assertions are difficult to accept, and I say that as a person who owns multiple Ouija boards and tarot decks. But even if we dismiss his claims that humans can develop paranormal abilities, his core premise strikes a vein of truth. We are too focused on measurable figures and statistics to understand life's ephemeral elements, magic or otherwise. In one of his easier-to-believe anecdotes, Wilson illustrates the utility of allowing occult forces and sensitivities into our lives. He describes a man on a morning walk in India who is struck with a deep-rooted compulsion to suddenly cross to the other side of the road. Disturbed by the break in his routine, he returns later to examine the area he avoided, finding signs that a tiger had been there earlier just beyond the roadside brush. Something, perhaps the elusive Faculty X, alerted the man to the presence of a predator. If he ignored his impulse, he might have been cat food.

The skeptical mind will immediately object that nothing supernatural occurred to the man, that he simply noticed the signs of the tiger on a subconscious level. Wilson anticipates this and accepts that it may be the case. But he suggests that accepting our mind's ability to collate sensory stimuli into an unexplainable, lifesaving urge to cross the road is essentially the same as a preternatural talent. It's not measurable, it's not trainable in any way we know, and it's therefore easy to deny despite its uncanny utility.

I am sympathetic to the Faculty X explanation of the tiger parable, and I believe that John Stainton experienced an ominous dread before the filming of *Ocean's Deadliest*. Minutes before my father was shot in the chest, he and I stood at a literal crossroads. Both of us, having seen some of the poverty of Limon, felt a sense of guilt and wanted to return to the ship—a straight walk from where we stood. But to our left, we could see a wooden pier, framed by a brightly coloured municipal building and a verdant park shaded by a high canopy of palm trees. Dad asked if I wanted to check it out, and I remember my muscles tensing. A foreboding note on the air warned me against it. But I love the ocean, which I could see a sliver of, and I was wearing my karate tournament T-shirt. *I have a black belt*, I thought. *Whatever happens, I'll be safe.*

What a strange impulse to ignore. By now you know how the rest plays out. We proceeded to the pier, Dad was shot, I dragged him to safety. But that ominous feeling would haunt me enough to serve as the theme for countless therapy sessions and sleepless nights. Notebook after notebook of traumatic free-writing. The dread worked its way into monologues, plays, and essays like this.

"Did I know it was going to happen?" I once asked Mark, my cognitive behavioural therapist.

"Maybe you did," he said. Therapists, in my experience, are generally open to Faculty X.

"Then I should have listened to it. I could have prevented it."

"You can't prevent what happened."

Framing trauma as a foregone conclusion warped my experience and memory of the omen into a contradictory knot. I remembered feeling the sensation of doom, and then having it confirmed by the shooting. But what if the shooting was so traumatic that it recontextualized my memory, adding the premonition into a less fortuitous crossroads event? What if there was no omen? Maybe I only remember my dread this way because I know what happens next.

"So what?" my therapist said. "You are here now. This isn't a vision of the future. You aren't stuck in the past. Omen or not, it doesn't change the present."

But it did change the present. Our conversation was proof of that. Which raises the question of just how far-reaching an omen can be. What if that spectral sign I sensed at the Limon crossroads was pointing even further down the path I chose to walk? Maybe the shooting was a speed bump and I'm still hurtling toward a dead end.

SPRING IS A HEARTBREAKING time at Australia Zoo. Located on Steve Irwin Way, the commercial nature conservatory—owned and operated by Terri Irwin with her children Bindi and Robert—is a massive tourist destination. Open daily from nine to five, the zoo's mission is in line with the departed Crocodile Hunter's conservation awareness strategy. You can sit in the bleachers of the Crocoseum (which is exactly what it sounds like) and watch Robert clown around with deadly lizards. You can explore the grounds and visit Komodo dragons, Tasmanian devils, Sumatran elephants, and a Burmese python. You can have your wedding on-site, or buy your infant child something called a "Cake Smash Photoshoot Package," in which they have a birthday party with star tortoises and echidnas. All of this entertainment serves as popular education, and also raises money for crocodile research, the Wildlife Warriors conservation program, and the zoo's twenty-four-hour emergency wildlife hospital, which gets particularly active between September and March.

As the weather heats up, animals start to move. They look for water, shade, mates, shelter. But their natural environment has been transformed by a web of human infrastructure. Roads, power plants, skyscrapers, and homes all increase the number of violent wildlife encounters with human beings. Kangaroos and wallabies hit by pickup trucks, koala joeys scorched in megafires, echidnas with broken limbs, crocodiles confused and angry as they guard swimming pools. The swift parrot, with its green coat, yellow breast, and red plumage around its delicate beak, colliding with a newly cleaned floor-to-ceiling window. No longer noisy. No longer nomadic. The species population ticks closer to zero. Welcome to Australia's trauma season.

The term trauma season is also used in North America, but in a different context. Healthcare workers here define the temporal window of violence based on human activity. With nicer weather and longer days, we venture out from the safety of our homes. We bike and swim and stay out late. We explore new places with new people. And we encounter danger. A stingray near the reef, a tiger in the bush, a man on the pier with a gun. In this way, trauma is elemental.

It's a storm we can measure only in its casualties after it has passed. Like all severe weather, thanks to the climate crisis, trauma season is getting longer. If only we'd seen the signs and trusted our faculties before this violent path was set, back when the forecast had time to change.

PAUL McCARTNEY'S
DECAPITATED HEAD IN THE BARDO

AS I WRITE THIS sentence in early 2023, Paul McCartney is still alive. But in the late 1960s, Beatles fans and conspiracy theorists around the world believed he'd been decapitated in a car accident. Imagine that: after an argument with his bandmates, he drove too fast, crashed, and lost his head. Picture that fab noggin, containing one of the great artistic minds of the twentieth century, flying through the air in slow motion. Macca's soft face gone slack, his gentle eyes vacant, his medium-long hair flipping back as his skull spins on its own axis.

It was impossible to prove Paul was alive, Ringo Starr says in *The Beatles Anthology*. The evidence was too elusive. According to the urban legend, after the traffic collision beheaded their bassist, Lennon, Harrison, and Starr replaced him with a lookalike named Billy Shears. Wracked with guilt, the surviving band left breadcrumbs for true believers. "Strawberry Fields Forever" contained a backwards confession, "I buried Paul." The dead man's doppelgänger wore a black carnation during the "Your Mother Should Know" scene in *Magical Mystery Tour*, while the others had red flowers. And he was the only Beatle in bare feet walking across the front of *Abbey Road*.

Even Paul himself couldn't demystify reports of his death. During the height of the rumour, he described a sensation of feeling transparent when he spoke to people, as if they were looking through him. McCartney was a ghost to everyone who didn't know him personally. It was just too easy to conjure the image of his headless shoulders.

THERE'S NO EASY WAY to admit this, but in the last few days of 2006 I thought I was dead. It started as a suspicion. The morning after Dad's shooting, I woke in my cabin to the sound of bells ringing. It was the PA system—our cruise director paging a woman to the guest services desk in the lobby. I got dressed. My bloody clothes from the day before were still being washed somewhere deep in the ship, but a stain on my shoe served as enough evidence to prove the violent encounter wasn't a nightmare. I made my way up to the Lido Deck to find we'd arrived in Panama.

Coffee and danishes for breakfast. Then I joined Nick, Mom, and Dad at an open-air table near the pool, and vacation continued as if the world had amnesia. The day before, when Mom and Nick returned from their ziplining excursion, they found Dad and I drinking in the light of the sunset. He and I kept the shooting a secret until dinner. At our table in the Silver Olympian Restaurant, Dad unbuttoned his shirt, revealing his wound. I broke down crying. Mom fainted. Nick laughed in surprise and caught her. When she came to, we drank together, and celebrated the good fortune of staying alive. It felt like a wake without a body. Later, Nick and I shared a smoke near the ship's bow, then collapsed in our beds. The holiday reset itself while we slept. I don't know what I expected—everyone survived, so why not continue to revel in luxurious recreation? Unlimited sun, food, drink, and leisure time ought to feel like a just reward after saving a life. But behind all the colours, flavours, and music, I felt immersed in the atmosphere of an abattoir.

The morbid ambiance followed me off the ship. We disembarked as a family. Panama, the final destination on our cruise itinerary, was billed as heaven for shoppers. Suits, scarves, tapestries, cigars, the famous brimmed hats—all the messaging around me hyped the commercial decadence of the port. But we were kept corralled with the rest of the cruisers in a concrete cul-de-sac marketplace with a handful of storefronts and a guarded gate beyond which taxis idled. Access to the indulgence we'd been promised was exclusively for passengers with planned excursions. The place felt incomplete. But I went through the motions and shopped, letting my existential paranoia simmer.

I bought a small souvenir guitar at a discount. It was missing a string. Maybe I could still tune it and play some songs. Calm my nerves. After forty minutes in the cordoned-off Panamanian lot, my family returned to the *Liberty*, where the announcement from earlier repeated intermittently. Can the woman we paged before please come to the guest services desk in the atrium of the Lobby Deck?

Rumours were spreading already. Something bad happened. After a shower back in my cabin, I returned to the open air and found Mom and Dad in a sunny corner of the Panorama Deck with a bucket of ice and cans of beer. Nick sat nearby, reading his powder-blue paperback collection of Arthur Rimbaud's poetry. I tried to tune the guitar. Pluck, pluck, plucking the string, twisting the machine head.

"People are saying she didn't come back yesterday," said Dad.

Ping, ping, ping, I tightened the string. If I could get the A and the E in tune, then I could at least play power chords.

"Maybe she went overboard," said Mom. "Do you think that's what happened?"

Pang. The A string snapped. I don't know what I expected—it was a toy guitar with mix-and-matched plastic and metal strings. Setting it down on the deck's warm wooden planks, I lay back in my pool chair, looked out at the inaccessible cityscape beyond, and hit play on my iPod. The 2006 Beatles mashup remix album *Love* piped into my ears. *This,* I thought, *is what it's like to be dead.*

LOVE IS HOLLOW. Mixed by famous producer George Martin and his son Giles expressly for the purpose of underscoring a Beatles-themed Cirque du Soleil production, the record is something of an abomination. Eighty-six minutes of time-skipping references to the better, original versions of songs like "Get Back," "Because," "Here Comes the Sun," and "Octopus's Garden," the album feels like a colourful facade. I bought the CD because at that point in my life I had never enjoyed the Beatles—with the exception of a few George songs—and I expected a polished remix would help me finally connect with their music. But what I got with *Love* was terminally lacking in context.

The day after Panama, as the *Liberty* waded along its two-day journey back to Fort Lauderdale, I strolled through the ship's corridors, listening to *Love* on repeat with the distinct impression something was missing. The music was arranged as a soundtrack, so it implied a complementary visual aspect. This was most apparent in the Frankenstein-ed track "Being for the Benefit of Mr. Kite!/I Want You/Helter Skelter," which seemed purpose-built for a high-flying trampoline act. The whole record evoked something more—a proper and complete whole reality—but all I had were its derivative symbols. Popular songs and iconic lyrics, begging me to recall their implied whole and historical importance, all of which was inaccessible in the middle of the ocean.

My environment was just as hollow as the music. The *Liberty* did its best impression of Las Vegas at sea. Every night there was a musical theatre review in the Venetian Palace, a proscenium theatre with three levels of seating, where a company of singers and dancers ran through the hits without the context-giving narrative of a full play. Showgirls' kick lines, the opening number of *West Side Story*, "Seasons of Love" from *Rent*—all on the same stage, smashed together into an empty spectacle. A collage without a theme. The twenty-four-hour buffet, the heat, the alcohol, the expectation of indulgence—it all whispered Nevada. But nothing truly captured the level of symbolic abstraction on the *Liberty* like the casino on the Promenade Deck: Czar's

Palace, a reference to Caesar's Palace in Las Vegas so closely linked semiotically that I get the impression the cruise line wants you to pronounce it "C-Zar's Palace."

Las Vegas is already derivative of all world history, and that makes it tricky to replicate. Sin City has a small version of the Eiffel Tower, captive dolphins in one of the casinos, and the famous Caesar's Palace echoes the home of Emperor Augustus. Imitating Vegas, the *Liberty* is a copy of a copy. Why see the world when you can go to Vegas, and why go to Vegas when you can wander a cruise ship?

Strolling through the shops just beyond Czar's Palace, I entered the balcony of the Venetian Palace theatre and sat alone in one of its cushioned seats. I brought with me a red hardcover journal—a notebook I used for composing theatre school monologues—and began pouring out my paranoia under the title: "Reasons I Know I'm Dead." The list was weird and rambling, but its conclusion seemed inescapable. My environment was a hollow reflection of symbols from my expired life, and I was either dreaming my final dream or experiencing a version of purgatory that was indistinguishable from that kind of death hallucination.

PICTURE PAUL MCCARTNEY'S HEAD again, still suspended in midair, moving in ultra slow motion. Undetectable movement, like it's frozen. His brain activity is spiking. He has no connection to his heart or his spinal cord or his lungs. A heartthrob's skull in free fall. Popular science says that our bodies try to protect us from the worst pain of death by sending us into a hallucinogenic dream state, one so intense that it might be indistinguishable from reality. And since those terminal dreams are endless, because decapitated Beatles don't wake up, Paul's head might experience an entire lifetime before it joins the burning wreck of his crashed car. He could live a thousand lives in those last airborne moments. Living the dream, dying again, only to be reborn. Day after day after day in the life. And who's to say whether, in his recursive death dream world, that Paul is always Paul? Maybe he's someone else. Maybe he's everyone else.

IN HIS SHORT STORY "Of Course It Is," Chuck Klosterman presents a narrator who is convinced of his own purgatorial state. He doesn't remember who he is or how he died, and the space around him doesn't seem to hold any significance beyond its repetition. Every day is the same for the anonymous protagonist. He wakes up, gets out of bed, checks the ID in his wallet to learn his name. The weather is perfect. He goes to a Chinese restaurant for lunch, then a record store with an incredible inventory where he buys some LPs. Heads to a bar to drink, watch basketball, and fall in love with the bartender who looks like Winona Ryder. He goes home where he finds delicious stew in his fridge he has no memory of making, which he eats, before going to bed and suddenly becoming aware he's stuck in a loop.

It's hell. Of course it is. Or at least it's purgatory, which according to the modern Catholic Church is as far from heaven as human souls can get, so it might as well be the bad place. Klosterman's story is an elegant picture of how the existential death-dream scenario is a foregone conclusion.

It's a genre of afterlife we are so familiar with that it's unremarkable.

When you're stuck in this type of existential hell, awareness of your circumstance is suffering. This has been the case for decades. In *Waiting for Godot*, Vladimir breaks out of his absurd comic loop with a self-aware monologue that betrays the play's secret horror. In Sartre's *No Exit*, the characters remember their lives and realize they exist to punish each other in hell's hotel lobby. In "Of Course It Is," the narrator is tortured by his own analysis of the cliché in which he is trapped.

The agony doesn't stop at mere awareness. The existential pain of these weird hells runs on an engine of purposeless analysis. In Klosterman's inferno, it's the questions raised by small details that haunt the punished soul, and the out-of-reach itch of an unsolvable puzzle is passed on to the reader. The effect is maddening, because you understand the *what* and the *where*, but never the *why*. You have all the symbols and can scrutinize them for eternity, but perpetual examination without conclusion is death.

The perfect detail that contributes to the story's infernal engine is the narrator's full awareness of popular culture. He naturally assesses the rarity of Miles Davis and Black Sabbath records, he recognizes NBA players on TV, and compares the beautiful bartender to Winona Ryder. Yet he can't remember his own name. This feels like a clue in solving his death mystery, but it's a dead end. Winona is a symbol, like everything else, closer to a place or thing than person. Celebrities mean something, but they can also mean anything, which in a way makes them meaningless. Glass onions that shift their significance depending on the angle you look at them. This is why some people don't believe Paul McCartney when he says he's alive. Macca, Ryder, all the people you only know from magazines and entertainment news—they are just more chains that keep us in analytical hell.

Lying in the twin bed of my interior cabin, I worried about what would happen if I, a dead teenager, fell asleep. So instead of closing my eyes I reread the non-fiction book I brought with me: *Chuck Klosterman IV*, a collection of the author's journalism and essays, culminating with a novella I had been saving for later. I reread chapters, searching for clues supporting my ghastly circumstances. An essay chronicling ex-members of the Beatles shined with new significance, given how much I was listening to *Love*. But that was nothing compared to an essay called "That '70s Cruise," in which Klosterman chronicles his own experience of a Carnival ship.

The essays twisted my mind into a feedback loop. The more I considered Klosterman's writing, the more I couldn't tell if it was the source of my death hallucination or a product of it. Did I read *IV*, die, and then inhabit aspects of the book, or did I die and imagine a book filled with the symbols I was surrounded with when I perished? I imagined my corpse. All the places it could be. Bloated and pickling in the dark Atlantic Ocean. Shattered and misshapen at the foot of the piano in the Lobby Deck after a three-storey fall through the atrium. Punctured and bleeding on the wooden pier in Costa Rica, next to the body of my own dead father, victims of a slightly more violent encounter with a stranger than I remembered.

Earlier that year I learned about Cotard's syndrome from

Klosterman's travel memoir *Killing Yourself to Live*. It's a condition where you think you're dead, and sometimes even smell your own rotting flesh. I thought about that passage and wondered if it was also a figment of my imagination. After all, here I was, travelling, journalling, thinking I was dead. I couldn't smell my corporeal decomposition, but maybe I would eventually. In the belly of the *Liberty*, in the middle of the ocean, in bed but wide awake, I was discovering the proximity between critical thought, paranoia, and death. It turns out there's a lot of overlap.

"BARDO MEANS GAP," says Chögyam Trungpa Rinpoche in his 1971 lecture on *The Tibetan Book of the Dead*, in which he seeks to give modern context to the verses spoken to dying Buddhists as they move through the six stages between life and the beyond. "It is not only the interval of suspension after we die but also suspension in the living situation; death happens in the living situation as well."

Trungpa Rinpoche describes the bardo experience as a common occurrence, not exclusive to the dead and dying, that includes "experiences of paranoia and uncertainty in everyday life; it is like not being sure of our ground, not knowing quite what we have asked for or what we are getting into." When I read this, presented as commentary in my Shambhala Pocket Library edition of *The Tibetan Book of the Dead: The Great Liberation through Hearing in the Bardo*, I think about falling. I think about my friend Josh, who killed himself in 2006 by jumping off a bridge. And because I think about Josh, I think about the tarot.

Josh died near the end of the winter semester. After a lifetime of Easter Mass, all the tulips and birdsong in the world can't hide spring's aura of death. I was preparing my audition for the second-year collective creation courses in my theatre program. A week before the performance, I got the call from a mutual friend, cried all night, and took the Greyhound back home. I put on the black suit I wore to my grandad's funeral two years earlier and carpooled to Josh's service with an old friend from high school. After the cremation, we sat in our formal wear in a vinyl-upholstered booth at the local Pizza Hut across from the mall. I can't remember what we talked about.

When I got home, I wrote my audition piece. The tryout required each applicant to write and perform a monologue based on one of the tarot's major arcana—twenty-two cards that hold significant spiritual meaning. My monologue came out as repeated song lyrics at first—Modest Mouse lines, poetry from slower Metric songs—and then I fixated on the image of a bridge. What was it like for Josh, on the edge before the fall? Was this the Tower, a symbol of catastrophe depicting figures surrounded by flame and rubble in freefall? Was this Death, the image of a skeletal knight standing among corpses, ignoring the pleading cries of his next victim?

Judgment was the card I chose. Finality. It depicts the Archangel Raphael, blowing into his apocalyptic horn, raising the dead from their watery graves. The bodies are grey and exalting, arms raised to the heavens. The event had happened, Josh's free fall had ended on the concrete asphalt. There was no bargaining. All that remained was a re-grounding and the dawn of what comes next.

My audition was Easter Monday. I stood before a panel of

course instructors and a crowd of fellow auditionees. I felt the floor beneath me, and I told them about what it means to be alive after someone you love dies. I exited the bardo of grief that day, and in the autumn—after my acceptance but before my time on the *Liberty*—the course instructor told us a trick.

"Don't get too in your head. Stay in your body. Every day, if you find yourself in patterns of repetition—if you are working the same shifts at your job, seeing the same people, taking the same bus routes and walking the same paths to the same lecture halls—this is your homework. Make it your mission to notice something new in the familiar. You are never stuck in the same place. You are always moving, you are always in transition. And if you can see that—the one detail that might have always been there, but it's new to you—then you can see the essence of life, which we want to capture and share with the world through what we make together in this classroom."

ON THE STARBOARD SIDE of the Promenade Deck, in the gap between Czar's Palace and the aft atrium, which was a sort of bar annex filled with different lounges, I sat at a table next to the window in the Jardin Café. My iPod kept playing *Love* as I continued my death journal and sipped another latte. It was daytime at sea, so I was alone, save for the barista behind the counter, with its silver espresso machine and glistening pastries. Everyone else was gambling or drinking or soaking up rays on the sunnier decks. Lido. Panorama. Spa. Sun and Sky. By then I wasn't thinking about them. This entire vacation was all a dream in my soon-to-be decomposing brain, so they probably weren't even real.

The bells kept chiming on the PA. The missing woman was still needed at the front desk. I thought about her, and whether she had plummeted from the *Liberty* into the turbulent ocean. How long did that fall take? Did she experience a purgatorial reverie? Or maybe she was just a symbol of my dying consciousness. I thought of Josh. I thought of the shooting. I wanted to cry but felt separated from my body. My theatre instructors would tell me to breathe. But I couldn't see the point. Not yet.

Eventually, every bardo has its end. The *Liberty* docked in Florida, and I returned to theatre school, where I came to see my deathly episode as the transition it was. A bizarre episode of shock-induced paranoia, sustained by limitless caffeine and the bright, hollow engine of derivative experience. On dry land I noticed new details in the familiar. I bought real Beatles CDs. Paul's head was no longer spinning. It never even left his shoulders. Billy Shears was imaginary, and I was as alive as McCartney.

But that all happened later. From my seat in the Jardin, I stared out the window at the blue-on-blue horizon where the sky pressed into the ocean. No ground in sight. Putting down my pen, I closed my red notebook, and opened *Chuck Klosterman IV* to the novella, marked by the section title "Something That Isn't True at All." I thought it might help me find something new in the familiar. The PA bells rang through the ship's speakers. In the climax of the story, as the protagonist drives to work on the highway, a woman falls from the sky and lands on the hood of his car. The woman is unidentifiable. She is dead. And maybe even dreaming.

A COIN IN THE EYE

I'M REMINDED OF AHAB and Mulder. Trauma gives you monster-vision, but it comes at a price. The white whale takes your leg. The aliens abduct your sister right before your eyes. And you become obsessed. You chase the leviathan to the end of the earth. You dedicate your life to discovering the truth about UFOS. You see yourself as the owner of the beast born of personal pain, but the creature is wild and untameable. Moby-Dick is as definitive to Ishmael as he is to Ahab. Scully is a victim of the aliens who turned Mulder into a paranoiac. My father was scarred by a bullet, but it changed my life too. No matter how personal your relationship to trauma feels, it's just as important to someone else. Try not to get jealous.

I'M REMINDED OF THE Citytv news story, though I can't bring myself to watch it. A short segment featured Dad, revealing the still-red scar on his chest, in which I was described simply as his son. The news crew came to my parents' place while I was attending school in Toronto and having my first flashbacks. They shot footage in the main hall, and near the kitchen table, and at the family computer. B-roll showed a map of Limon, the cruise line website, mouse clicks, keystrokes. The reporter's voiceover told a story, but not mine. My father, shown safe at home, was in Costa Rica with his son when they were mugged. The man on TV was shot. And now he wants to warn other vacationers to be careful during this particularly violent travel season. He's not the only one—you could be next.

They found my monster and turned it into a learning opportunity. It had value to the news producers, and it had value to my father, but I didn't recognize it as my experience. This was not the great white shark terrorizing my beaches. This was not the barbarian wreaking havoc on my abandoned suburban neighbourhood at night. I was happy Dad got his message out and I hoped the news segment would help spare other vacationers from disaster. But while the news was accurate and well intentioned, I felt written out of my own story.

I'M REMINDED OF "Who Is the Bad Art Friend?" by Robert Kolker, an essay published in the *New York Times* chronicling the dispute between writers Dawn Dorland and Sonya Larson over who owns whose trauma. The article, published in October 2021, is expertly constructed as an elevated Am I the Asshole? Reddit post, asking readers to pick a side in a dispute of manners. Dorland, whom Kolker describes as having an "un-self-conscious earnestness that endears her to some people and that others have found to be a little extra," donated her kidney to a non-directed recipient. Larson was inspired by the donation and Dorland's subsequent extra-ness—celebrating a kidney-versary, marching in parades, and posting to Facebook a letter addressed to the eventual recipient of her organ—and so she wrote a story about it. But she didn't tell Dorland, whose behaviour served as a model for Larson's antagonist.

The supposed badness of these art friends hinges on a litany of cringe-inducing offences. Dorland's earnestness comes off as self-righteous and void of irony in Kolker's essay. Larson and her friends have their private messages mocking Dorland subpoenaed—a scenario so exquisitely awkward it's the basis for a sketch on the cringe-comedy revue *I Think You Should Leave with Tim Robinson*. Larson's depiction of Dorland is critical of the donor's supposedly altruistic motivations, and by the end of Kolker's essay, I got the impression that the story was made at least partially to ridicule the woman. Dorland, on the other hand, dedicates a significant amount of time and money pursuing the copy-right on her donor letter—which is directly quoted in the story—and getting Larson dropped from prestigious read-ing events. Lawsuits. Countersuits. Allegations of stalking. Accusations of defamation and white saviourism. And it all comes down to your judgment as the reader: Who is worse?

But another person appropriated Dawn Dorland's altru-istic nephrectomy—Kolker's essay has easily become the definitive framing of the conflict—and now I feel a bleeding sympathy for both women. I know what it's like to define myself around a single event. Yet even in this very book, I am just as much a Larson: ripping stories of true crime and violence from the news, from the lives of family and friends, to highlight how other peoples' worst days support my own machinations.

I'm not qualified to be on this jury. If Kolker's question of writing community etiquette comes down to the behaviour of Dawn Dorland or Sonya Larson, then I must throw myself on the mercy of the court. It's me: I'm the bad art friend.

I'M REMINDED OF JORDAN PEELE'S *Nope*, which begins with Hollywood horse trainer OJ Haywood trying to save the life of his father, Otis Sr., who had an American quarter shoot through his eye and lodge in his brain. Otis dies in the hospital, and the image of his final X-ray—a skull with a coin in the eye socket—looms over the proceeding story about trying to make a buck from the wild phenomenon that is violent trauma.

The killer quarter ended up in Otis's eye on a freak accident, propelled by a skyborne beast that happens to perfectly resemble a classic flying saucer straight out of a 1950s sci-fi flick. The cryptid is more akin to a people-eating jellyfish than a spaceship, careening through the desert air using self-generated electromagnetic waves, heralded by the screams of its latest meal—humans and horses awaiting digestion. OJ and his sister, Emmy, uncover the monster and seek to photograph it. Fully aware that UFO videos aren't exactly rare in the era of YouTube and government declassification, the Haywoods are aiming for the Oprah shot: irrefutable photographic evidence and their ticket to financial stability.

By virtue of their father's death, the predator in the clouds feels like the Haywoods' property. They even name it Jean Jacket, after a horse that has traumatic significance to Emmy. But their neighbour, former child actor turned theme park owner Ricky "Jupe" Park, has also staked a claim, draping his own violent memories on Jean Jacket like so much emotional bunting.

To see Jean Jacket through Jupe's framing is to see an entirely different monster. Jupe is the sole unscathed survivor of a brutal chimpanzee attack on the set of a 1990s sitcom called *Gordy's Home*. He co-starred alongside a trained ape wearing human clothes. While filming an episode about Gordy the chimp's birthday, a balloon popped on set, driving the animal into a frenzy. Gordy pounded and bit and tore apart his castmates, the film crew, and the live studio audience. He draped the set in gore and ripped the face off the other child star, Mary Jo Elliott. When Gordy found Jupe hiding under a table, he reached out his knuckles to tap them against his only friend, but before they made contact, a rescue team blew Gordy away with a shotgun.

"That's the world's first exploding fist bump," Jupe tells the Haywoods, pointing to a framed still on the wall of a hidden exhibit built in tribute to the *Gordy's Home* incident. Normally Jupe charges money for people to see the shrine of his trauma, a white room filled with recovered paraphernalia, including Mary Jo Elliott's bloodstained shoe and Gordy's birthday hat. He has made the incident proprietary despite coming away with his face intact. But he is unsatisfied. By his own admission, a *Saturday Night Live* sketch parodying the worst day of his life, starring Chris Kattan as Gordy, told the story best. Jupe can hoard souvenirs of his trauma, but he can't fully own the event that haunts his daydreams.

Jupe wants his trauma to be his alone. So, when the apex predator in the sky shows up, he sees an opportunity to extend the commodification of his painful narrative by building a ticketed outdoor sideshow around it—luring the creature from the clouds to an amphitheatre with the promise of tasty horses. He creates a mythology for the flying saucer, inventing little alien mascots whose faces evoke the image of Gordy. Dressing the beast in images of his own pathos, Jupe stakes his claim.

Between the Haywoods and Jupe, we see two traumas pinned to the same monster, and two methods of trying to exploit it. Emmy Haywood eventually photographs Jean Jacket using a novelty camera built into a well at Jupe's theme park. The former child star is not so lucky. In trying to dominate the avatar of his most terrible memories, Jupe finds himself outmatched. Jean Jacket descends from the sky and, like Gordy before him, chases down the gawking audience who would make a spectacle of it and tears them apart.

I'M REMINDED OF THE makeshift confessional in my elementary school gymnasium, where three priests served as God's referees, doling out penalties to sinful children. It never occurred to me then, but those priests, sitting in green plastic chairs under a large wooden crucifix in a basketball-proof Plexiglas box, heard multiple stories originating from the same events. Singular encounters created a multitude of debts among the student body.

When something is wrong, we make it better by telling a story. We confess, we write, we document, we pray. It's supposed to be cleansing, not competitive. After each session, a guilty student knelt at a table in centre court, bearing a statue of Mary where we'd have tipoff during basketball games. I couldn't help but glance at the giant scoreboard behind the Mother of God as I recited my assigned penance. Usually the board was blank, but occasionally it lit up and the score was nil. Two giant zeroes, one for the home team and one for visitors.

EIGHT SUCCESS SECRETS FOR THE TRAUMATIZED SERVICE WORKER

1. Don't Answer Your Employer When He Calls You with Your Schedule

The obvious steps are always the most valuable. You need time to get your bearings, so don't answer your goddamn phone. Just stare at it, vibrating in your hand, displaying the first name of the man who manages the Second Cup where you work. Delete the voice mail he leaves for you without listening to it. This is a surefire way for your manager to assume something very bad happened to you when you were away on a family vacation.

Don't worry if it feels unnatural at first. You'll have plenty of opportunities to perfect this technique. Omar is going to call you for weeks, maybe even months. If your phone is still active it means you're paying your phone bill, so what's up? He wants to know.

2. Deliver Dramatic News in Person

You are going to need a job eventually. Here's a little life hack for you: there's one waiting for you at Second Cup. That's why your phone is still ringing. But after all that time neglecting Omar, you're better off missing the call and delivering the dramatic news in person.

Important news requires a full-system approach—you need body language and that weird tense aura that emanates from humans in crisis to properly sell your inability to answer your phone. That way, when you walk into the back room of the Second Cup to find Omar working on the payroll in the same cold room where he stores vacuum-packed silver bean bags of coffee, he can tell from your posture that something bad *did* happen. Once he sees you, tell him about the shooting you witnessed. Tell him how you haven't been sleeping. Tell him you're sorry you didn't return his calls.

Omar will hug you, despite your deep slouch and vacant pin-dot eyes, and you will have completed secret number two. Congratulations, enjoy the powerful new scent memory: associating Second Cup's signature Paradiso blend with compassion.

3. Hustle the Pain Away

While you were avoiding Omar's calls, you probably ran out of money, and because it was easier to start over fresh, you went to the rich people mall and handed out resumés with your best friend. When you're called by the fancy chocolate store in the mall, take the job and balance it with your barista gig. If for no other reason than this: customer-facing work forces you out of the post-traumatic mindset. You're not allowed to express emotions in front of management or customers. That level of discipline and dissociation is near impossible to achieve without tangible threats to your minimum-wage livelihood.

Your chocolate store job is with a Belgian confectionary chain that sells extremely expensive chocolate. The store has two walls made entirely of glass. Employees joke that it's a snow globe filled with sweets. Your job's location is heavily surveilled by the district manager, Kelly, who, rumour has it, acquired her infamous peppy aggression during time served as an army drill sergeant. Her reputation of spying on the store from a distance and cataloguing your behaviour precedes her. She camps out behind the sale rack in the adjacent Harry Rosen, or just out of view near the Bentley luggage showroom.

Kelly counts the number of customers entering the store and times how long it takes them to exit. Are you handing out samples to mall walkers? Are you engaging them in a descriptive sales pitch, divulging the store's rich history and describing the candy like a fine wine? When you're in the chocolate theatre—a marble fixture with two inset chocolate fountains located in the corner where the glass walls meet—how sensual are your dips? Are you making a show of picking the most luscious strawberries before you lower them into molten chocolate and pull them out with a flourish, magically increasing their per-piece value beyond what you make in an hour? Don't answer; if she's dissatisfied, you'll hear about it. But not necessarily on the same day. Kelly will voice her ire to your manager over the phone, or on the next time she has an official scheduled store visit. You are always under scrutiny, and scrutiny drives hustle.

But head office isn't the most demanding force at the store. The customer base are your real bosses. And not just the data-collecting secret shoppers hired by corporate to mine detailed customer-service analytics. Each regular customer at your store has their own standards that you must learn through trial, error, and oral tradition among staff. That eight-year-old using a credit card to buy a ten-dollar glazed apricot dipped in milk chocolate? Technically it's against store rules to let him make a non-cash purchase. It might even be illegal. But his short dad is always looking for an excuse to flirt with your seventeen-year-old co-workers, and if you deny the kid's purchase, the father will come in to scream at you and then demand free candy. The ancient lady who always complains about the store's exorbitant prices? That's just how she talks. Part of her weekday routine is taking a tour of the snow globe and berating "you people" for gouging her, before buying over a hundred dollars of bonbons.

If you're really lucky, you'll have a customer like Mr. Havisham. At first you'll hear him whispered about, or you'll come in on Wednesday and see a colleague with dried tear tracks dividing her face into columns. Then maybe you flip to the wrong section in the binder where you log your hours and see a multi-page section with the heading "HAVISHAM ORDER." Pages and pages of product names—champagne truffle, crème brûlée, milk chocolate vanilla caramel—with numbers beside them.

When you meet Havisham at first, he looks like a potato in a windbreaker. And he's not scary. He's kind. It's difficult to understand how this guy inspired your manager to have several mild panic attacks over the size of the strawberries in his order. She hands him two large gift bags filled with three hundred dollars' worth of hand-packed boxes of chocolate. Their interaction is jovial. Your manager says something like, "Everything else was perfect, so we're probably in the clear."

An hour passes. Maybe an hour and a half. And the phone rings.

"What the hell are you trying to pull? Is the order unclear?"

He doesn't even care about the size of the berries. Apparently it's the orientation of the champagne truffles. You relay this to your manager and tell her Mr. Havisham is on his way. When he shows up, he apologies for being stern on the phone. It's not his order. The woman he works for, she's the unreasonable one. But please help him put the truffles in the right positions so everyone can be happy.

The hustle numbs the PTSD, so you want to keep it up, and the secret to success is right there in the job description: customer service. The customer might not always be right, as the retail maxim goes, but you're paid to serve them. Each one is a mad king or queen, and you are their serf. You need to dance to their exacting expectations, which must be intuited through careful observation. And that all-encompassing demand, powered by the high stakes of living on extremely low wages, pushes your own pain out of frame. Smile and greet the customer, dip the strawberries with a flourish while wearing a humiliating paper chef's hat. Know you are being watched and judged. Make it matter. That's how you quiet your deeper suffering. It could be worse, after all—at least these shoppers aren't trying to shoot you and your dad. Be grateful.

4. Cry in Front of Assistant Managers, Not Managers
Your hustle is noble and it will go a long way to building the customer service persona you depend on to hide from your trauma. But it isn't bulletproof. One day a kid will pop a balloon outside the store while you're filling a piping bag with milk chocolate and your eyes will begin to water. That's okay. It's all part of the lifestyle. Quickly but carefully empty the piping bag back into the fountain so that the chocolate doesn't harden. Then, briskly walk back to the closet behind the service counter where everyone keeps their coats and boots. Your ceaseless anxiety and dollar-value diet of tofu stirfry will help you fit back there.

Ideally, an assistant manager will find you. She will ask you what happened, and instead of saying a kid with a balloon shattered your sense of time and mortality, you start from the beginning of your new, abridged story. "I have PTSD from when I saw my dad get shot. I'm okay."

And you aren't okay, but you will be. Crying in front of an assistant manager builds sympathy, and sympathy waters down their worry of what your mental illness will do to the store's sales potential. You can't get fired for being mentally ill, but you can have your hours cut, and less time working is more time worrying. Besides, it's easier to trauma-bond with assistant managers. You will get drinks after that encounter and will make it a regular thing. You will call your after-work drinking "The Sad Bastards Club," and that's when you can see the truth of all this advice. It turns out your assistant manager is an orphan with her own grief and trauma. And to her, Mr. Havisham and the lesser dukes and duchesses of the rich people mall are also greater villains than the nightmare

monsters of real life. Chocolate problems are more immediate than existential problems, and your co-workers feel
this too.

5. Leave before Your Enemies Become Your Allies

The blood on Mr. Havisham's face is red and bright when
he tells you he's quitting. Scratches, probably. Human claws
ripped at his sweaty face in the time between his morning
visit to pick up the order and his inevitable return when
your chocolate configuration was not up to his employer's
impossible standards.

"She's gone too far," he says. Again and again. "Too far.
This time was too far."

You can't believe this is happening. Thankfully your
co-workers see it too. The man who terrorized you every
Wednesday for years is falling apart in the light of the truffle
display case.

"And don't help Sheila. Don't do it."

You thought Sheila was his assistant when she started
showing up every other Wednesday. Apparently she's his
replacement.

"This is it. I'm done."

Mr. Havisham will fade away and you'll get to know
Sheila, with her high and tight haircut and her easier relationship with the big boss, Margaret. Margaret will start
calling you directly when the order's messed up. It turns out,
she's more reasonable when you speak to her directly. Also,
it turns out that Mr. Havisham is her brother.

One morning, you will be crouched in front of the store,
unlocking the retractable gate at the start of your shift. You

will feel a warm hand pat your shoulder. Not threatening, but one of comradery. You'll turn around to find empty space. Looking in the direction of the mall exit, you'll see the unmistakable silhouette of your old oppressor, the potato man. Time to quit. Hang up your apron before your job becomes too comfortable to distract you from the pain it used to obscure.

6. Don't Pretend to Be Benjamin
By the time you get to this secret, chances are the economy is in a recession. Not an ideal time to be jobless. But you'll be fine. Just remember: you are not better than telemarketing. You might be scared of telemarketing, and you might be ill suited for telemarketing, but you are not above it. Phone-sales folks are just like you, trying to survive in a cruel world. On your journey, you will meet these kind-hearted touch-tone warriors—artists supporting themselves as they pursue acting, music, filmmaking, essay-writing.

Take the job selling opera subscriptions to the arts patrons of Toronto. You'll quickly learn that a few hundred dollars isn't a lot of money to some people. But that can be an obstacle at first: the easiest way to sell something is to understand why you would buy it, and no one at the call centre can afford a four-figure ticket to see *Rigoletto*. Another challenge is getting sworn at. Apparently, people think this is a totally normal thing to do. And as you discover, it's a slow trigger for PTSD.

Telemarketing is a difficult job, but outbound call centres are always hiring and they pay well enough. The reps who are best at it simply follow a script, which is a choose-your-own-adventure-style pamphlet designed to sell high-priced subscriptions and counter every possible objection to buying opera tickets. Some centres pay direct commission, but yours is a pro-rate system. If you hit certain goals, your hourly wage goes up. You also have a room sales goal, and if everyone works together to achieve it, you all get rewarded, sometimes with ice cream sandwiches.

Frozen confectionaries aside, telemarketing is pure, uncut Havisham-level customer service injected into your femoral artery. It's like having your eyelids pried open *Clockwork Orange*–style and being forced to behold all the worst behaviours nurtured in society.

You might feel shame as you pick up your first paper lead of the evening—name and number at the top, followed by opera-going history and notes from previous calls during previous phone campaigns. You might feel exhausted. You might get stage fright before manually punching a number into your black office phone. One week, after a particularly rough spate of customers, you might start introducing yourself as Benjamin. Benjamin is not real, an invention created to absorb the insults. Benjamin has endurance. Benjamin is that fucking worthless scum who should never call here again. Benjamin can't be on the brink of a post-traumatic breakdown, because Benjamin is just a name.

Your colleagues will mock you for this behaviour at first, but soon a few reps will try lying about their names too. It'll became a joke, and you'll find levity. Switching names, eating ice cream, talking to strangers about *Tosca* and *Madama Butterfly* and *Bluebeard's Castle*. But the hours will pass and Benjamin won't improve your sales. Best to abandon your alter ego before your manager shouts, "Last call."

For telemarketing to work, you have to accept you are not

above the task. This is your life, this is your job. Ice cream sandwiches are for closers, and you can't close if you don't believe in yourself.

7. Use Poor Sales Performance as an Excuse to Share Your Trauma

It's only a matter of time before some asshole who laughs at his own *Seinfeld* references breaks you. You recognize the joke, as you've heard a million dads do it on a million dinner-interrupting calls.

"Give me your number," he says. "I'll call you at home."

He wants you to protest. Like the telemarketer on the sitcom, setting him up for the punchline: "Now you know how I feel."

You persist without acknowledging the reference. You say this can take less than a minute. You can get him seats to all seven operas this season for practically nothing when you think about it. And then he swears at you. "Don't you fucking watch *Seinfeld?*"

Does this guy think you, as the butt of his interpretation of Jerry Seinfeld's decade-old joke, should be grateful? The answer is yes. You mean nothing to this man. It doesn't matter what you've been through or how much you're struggling. He doesn't care about the life you saved a few years ago. In fact, while his anger lingers around your cubicle like an acid rain cloud dissolving what's left of your resolve, he's probably already forgotten about you. He'll never think about you again, and if he does it will be as he retells the story of perfectly re-enacting that bit from *Seinfeld*, season four, episode three, "The Pitch."

Put the phone down. Get up. Go stand in your manager's office. Close the door. Tell her you're having trouble. You're slower than usual today because of your PTSD. That acronym always shocks people at first. But then they ascribe it to you as a label and it just becomes a category. As before, at the coffee shop and the chocolatier, tell the story. Say you were in Costa Rica, your dad got shot, you had to save his life, and it messed you up. Sometimes you have trouble focusing. You will still try but you are manoeuvring with difficulty.

The confession buys you freedom to call a little slower that night. Lets you log your hours at the base pay. But in the pure-results arena of an outbound call centre, a manager's understanding doesn't change the fact that you will only make enough money to live if you're able to convince people to see at least four operas next year.

You need money, and the harsh reality of capitalism makes no accommodation for mental anguish below the threshold of hospitalization. If you need to share your trauma for sympathy, that's all well and good, but it's not enough to get you out of work. Save it for your Sad Bastards Club.

8. Retraumatize Yourself at Every Opportunity

Your sales won't recover. Take a morning job at Starbucks to supplement your income, to pay your climbing rent. Tell them right away: "I have PTSD, it's not really a problem, but if it gets to be one, I'll let you know." Get up at 5:00 a.m. to open the store with the assistant manager, who is a DJ in her spare time, then work to 1:00 p.m., nap for a couple of hours on your twin bed in your midtown apartment, then trek downtown to sell operas from 5:00 p.m. to 10:00 p.m. As a balm between jobs, watch *Adventure Time*, a children's cartoon that has some nuanced commentary on trauma and grief, but is mostly an imaginative fantasy show about a boy and his magic dog.

The lack of sleep will wear on you, and in your darkest moments you'll receive a long-awaited call back from a job interview you had at the symphony. Take this job, answering phones instead of dialing them. Your telemarketing experience is an asset. People will phone you because they already decided they want you to sell them concert tickets. But triggers are everywhere, and eventually you'll find yourself in another manager's office, shrink-wrapped eyes, gaunt cheeks, telling your story in a bid for sympathy, worried about job performance.

Don't worry. You aren't that job's biggest liability. A load-bearing annual donation will fail to materialize, and you'll be out of work soon enough. Take up freelancing instead. Trade magazines are always hiring. Now *that's* a gig that requires a nonstop workaholic engine. By now you're prepared. The unforgiving hustle and insane demands of customer service has refined you into a machine. Online, they call this paradigm the grindset. In clinical terms, it's avoidance.

At lunches with clients, on video calls with long-term contract employers, you'll have to explain why you can't handle too much travel, especially to Las Vegas or other cruise ship–esque destinations. No one will know what to do when you tell them about your trauma. They'll get caught up in the strange gearshift between smiling business demeanour and cold sweat fear or confused sympathy. Helpless. But you hope they'll listen. You hope they'll remember. At least until you have a new job, where no one knows your pain, but everyone needs to hustle. Keep it up!

CYLONS

SCHMOOZING IN THE BRIGHT gallery, I felt like a Cylon, one of the robot villains from *Battlestar Galactica*. Throughout the show's run, they served as a complex metaphor for religious and political ideology in the post-9/11 era. Indistinguishable from humans until they're triggered, Cylons infiltrated society and lived among us. They were hidden terrorists. They were prisoners of war. They were torture victims. They were an occupying force. They were insurgents. They were the most trusted advisors on the titular spaceship, paranoid of themselves and what their nature might compel them to do. I related to that last part most. The moments of lonely crisis as characters who thought they were human grappled with the wireless signal telling them otherwise.

Emma was exhibiting a show with her graduate fine arts class—collectively they presented a series of fluxus scores, creating moments of interactivity and artistry. One of the scores was "Have a Party," so the artists dropped balloons from the ceiling. It was colourful and exciting. And then a couple professors started stomping on the red, yellow, and blue party favours. *Bang, bang, bang.* Each stamp a mock gunshot. Every pop a psychic shockwave. I saw the professors laughing—these guys had a reputation for trolling their sensitive students. My bones ached as I resisted their reflexive bending. My PTSD was coming online.

I knew the asshole professors expected attendees like me to explode. When I first started researching my condition online, I came across all kinds of mockery and hatred. On the same website I used to learn the name for what I was experiencing based on the symptoms it listed, I read that some people called it "NBD." No backbone disorder. Thinking I was suffering after achieving the heroic, I read something online saying I had a coward's disease. In the gallery, I was overwhelmed with that same scattershot ridicule.

I swore under my breath, suppressed the tremors in my joints, and told Emma I would be next door at the student bar. That's where the afterparty was being held. She understood, but couldn't join me. The school's president was in attendance, scheduled to make a speech addressing the MFA students, the board of directors, notable alumni, donors, and all the people who help keep the school running.

On television, PTSD is most overtly represented through negative depictions of triggering. In *Hannibal*, special agent Will Graham's triggers are manipulated by the cannibal psychiatrist to horrific and amoral ends. In *Lost*, Desmond Hume inadvertently breaks the heart of his soulmate through *Slaughterhouse-Five*–inspired post-traumatic time travel. Cylons set off nuclear explosives and extinguish human life.

When Principal Skinner is triggered by a Valentine's Day prank in the famous "I Love Lisa" episode of *The Simpsons*, his public experience of a Vietnam flashback is technically funny, especially to a member of the Bart Simpson generation. But the act of laughing at someone for having an experience I actively hide from the world feels like self-betrayal. Generally, Skinner can eat my shorts, but when he screams for his fallen squad-mate Johnny over the school PA system, I want to buy the yellow cartoon educator a drink.

I slipped away from the gallery, otherwise unnoticed. Dim light and soft music filled the nearly empty bar. Blissful negative space. I ordered a double Irish whiskey and sat next to another man, about my age, also hitting the liquor. He was ex-navy, I knew, and now a student at the school.

"It was getting to be a little loud in there," he said.

We shared a moment of silent recognition. We clinked glasses and sipped our drinks. We chose to remain human.

TINGLES GUARANTEED

Tap tap

The sensation starts at the top of your head, expands into a crown of gentle tingles, and spreads across your scalp before cascading down your body. It's euphoric. The tingles release tension and immerse you in a fog of sleepy relaxation. The effect is called ASMR, which stands for autonomous sensory meridian response, a pseudoscientific name for a real phenomenon. Comforting as it is, ASMR is mostly discussed reluctantly and with embarrassment, if at all. Many find the tingles too intimate.

Embraced by an enthusiastic YouTube community of teens, massage therapists, wellness professionals, e-mystics, internet sex workers, and musicians, ASMR is primarily conjured by audiovisual stimuli. Practitioners whisper into high-end microphones, tap different objects, click their tongues, and hypnotically move their hands in front of cameras, creating hours and hours of seemingly nonsensical video content. Some viewers trigger the sensation to help them sleep, others like to feel it when they work as a way to counteract stress and anxiety.

In a 2020 interview with *Pitchfork*, Phoebe Bridgers revealed that ASMR videos helped her write her highly acclaimed sophomore album *Punisher*. "Sometimes when I'm writing and I want something in the background, I'll put an ASMR video on really low," she told *Pitchfork*'s Quinn Moreland. "It gives you a brain fog and makes you fall asleep and you can get sucked into it, but also it stops you from listening to your life."

Tingly sounds are all around us. That's how I first discovered ASMR. Walking home from one of Emma's cello lessons, I asked her, "Have you ever noticed how calming your teacher's voice is? It's like he's tangibly making the air in the room heavier."

"That's a whole phenomenon," she said. "There's a specific term for it. Apparently people get it from watching Bob Ross painting videos."

A few years later, caught in the slow burn of a days-long PTSD episode, I remembered that cello lesson vibe. I googled "relaxing voice phenomenon," and a few clicks later I was treating my prickly hypervigilance with the soft-spoken words of a stranger on a webcam. It didn't completely douse my post-traumatic flare-up, but it dampened the heat. Soothing, but not a cure. "ASMR is not a replacement for clinical help," wrote the video's uploader in pre-emptive agreement, before printing a list of mental health resources.

The YouTube algorithm immediately started recommending new types of sound sessions. Intrepid tinglenauts searching for the next calming soundwave—tapping on exotic surfaces, contorting their mouths into novel shapes to produce a rare gurgle, finding obscure soft or slimy dollar-store toys to squeeze next to the mic, and creating elaborate role-playing scenarios to imitate incidental noises that produce tingles in the wild, like a doctor writing a prescription. Guided by the recommendation tray, I hopped from video to video in search of a reprieve from my shooting-induced PTSD symptoms. Before long, I found myself blissing out to a video of a young man whispering into a microphone in his bedroom while jiggling the slide of a Glock 22 he borrowed from his brother.

That weapon wiggler is YouTube's ASMR Rich, a twenty-something ASMRtist from Georgia, and when it comes to gun sounds for sleep and relaxation, he is a maestro. Whether it's gently tapping on a .40-calibre hollow-point bullet, sliding the magazine in and out of his handgun's handle, or whispering a freestyle rap before revealing he has a real rocket launcher, Rich never fails to get the tingles flowing. "I don't know how I'm about to do this," he says into the camera as he hoists the artillery onto his lap, "but I'm about to try and make this as relaxing as possible for y'all."

The fact that gun ASMR works is a miracle of semiotics and an absolute dream for fans of irony. In its purest form—gun sounds for relaxation videos with no talking, in which practitioners clean their weapons on camera without commentary—this subgenre of tingle video is also educational, showing viewers how to safely disassemble, wipe down, oil, and reassemble pistols of various sizes. Others, like those made by Rich, seem to revel in the absurdity of contradiction. A community of millions of viewers coming together to feel physical pleasure by watching a stranger fondle a tool made with the express purpose of killing human beings.

"As a gun guy in need of sleep," writes one commenter on a video of gun-cleaning sounds by user ASMRbyJ, "I loved this!!!"

Click click

Have you ever licked a nine-volt battery? Imagine that acid-sour tingle, but in your bones and muscles and behind your eyes, amplified sporadically. Have you ever daydreamed so hard that, despite your eyes being open, you actually lose your vision? Imagine that level of visual cortex stimulation, but completely involuntary and the reverie is a rerun. The first time I blacked out from a PTSD flashback, I was watching a preview performance of a short play by my theatre school classmates. The sixteen of us had been assigned groups and given the task of making a fifteen-minute play based on a painting. The group on stage took Banksy's Gaza Strip graffiti and turned it into a tight and entertaining dystopian crime thriller. After a double-cross was revealed, one actor pulled out a small black cap gun and pointed it at his scene partner.

Click. The cap didn't fire. I felt a stone of nausea in my diaphragm.

Click. To cover for the technical difficulty, the gunman started to scream.

Click. The battery acid. *Click.* The pinprick sweat. *Bang.* Lights out.

My friend Gabe found me shaking and crying in the hall outside our class studio.

"Are you okay?"

"I wish I knew it was loaded."

I returned to class, found my seat, and saw my open notebook defaced with my own jagged all-caps writing: PLEASE WARN BEFORE USING GUNS.

Bang bang

It's the smell I remember most. And the muted bang-bang-bangs of gun rapport through noise-cancelling ear protection. I thought it would make me crumple into a crying ball, the way fireworks and cap guns have in my most vulnerable moments. Or that it would flood my senses with an overwhelming torrent of adrenalin. But the sensation of firing a handgun feels great, and it's addictive.

"This might sound crazy," Alex said, "but holding a gun feels natural to me."

Our friend Susan was there too, and my brother. We sat with our drinks around a table at a Toronto pub called the Artful Dodger, a couple of hours after our field trip to the Range, a beginner-friendly shooting gallery located in Brantford, Ontario.

"That makes sense," I said. "It was easier than I expected."

"I would never do it again," said Susan. "The guns hurt my hands. It was loud. None of it was appealing at all. I'm glad you had a good time, though. But it was truly unpleasant."

"Our guys were good, though," said Nick. "I didn't expect our guys to be so nice."

We all agreed there. Tony and Kevin were our expert instructors and safety personnel. They met us in a fluorescent-lit lunchroom with interior windows overlooking the shooting lanes. Based on how the Range's website described this lounge area, I had expected something like a university ice rink restaurant. I hoped there would be fries. But it was just six tables, some chairs, and a vending machine. The arrhythmic discharge of gunfire crashed into me, and I suppressed my natural flinch reaction.

Kevin, the younger of the two guides, presented the safety instructions and then we were led into the shooting area. He stayed with Nick and Alex in a far lane. They'd signed up to shoot a variety of weapons, from small arms to semiautomatic machine guns, a sniper rifle, a massive shotgun, and the sci-fi–looking Kriss Vector 9mm. Susan and I were in the next lane over with Tony. We both opted to fire only handguns.

"There were so many shirts with slogans like 'ammo babe'—I was surprised they didn't have guns that fit your hands," Nick said.

"I just really wish they came in pink." Susan's smirk revealed her contempt for the whole activity. "Tony was nice, though. He kept telling me I was doing a good job. I just wanted to chase that approval."

I agreed. Tony guided me through a prix fixe menu of lead, giving me a tour of each pistol—its crosshairs, its ammo size, its unique hand-feel. If the gun was going to kick, he encouraged me to lean forward to absorb the recoil. For the semiautomatic SIG-320 RX, once I got the hang of it, he suggested I try rapidly firing a couple of rounds. *Try a double tap.* Each bullet made a hole in a sheet of paper with a target printed on it. When I got a bullseye, Tony would make sure I noticed. *Nice shot! Well done!* He encouraged me to savour the experience, and I did. I dined on ten rounds of a Glock 17, six of a Smith & Wesson .38 Special revolver, ten of the SIG with its super-accurate red dot sight, ten of a Glock 22, and a delicious eight .45 calibre rounds of a 1911. It's a cliché that high-calibre guns are more fun to shoot. I was embarrassed to find out it's true.

"If it didn't wear out my muscles, I could have gone broke buying more ammo," I said.

"Really?" asked Susan.

"It wasn't like I expected. I feel like I did a hundred push-ups. The adrenalin doesn't even feel addictive—I just wanted to get better. I'd probably feel the same way about archery."

We ordered food and more drinks. An unshaven man interrupted our conversation to tell us how provocative he found the work of George Orwell, then he put some loonies in the red-upholstered pool table. The sharp clink of the billiards balls tapped my eardrums with a manicured fingertip. PTSD nerves. Maybe the experience was a bit more upsetting than I was willing to admit.

"There was a part I found really scary," Nick said. "I was aiming with the semiautomatic rifle, and I had my finger on the trigger, and I thought it was just resting, and bang! It fired. I barely touched it."

"Yeah," said Alex. "When I went to order more ammo for the revolver, I mentioned to Kevin I was surprised to see you could just buy these high-powered weapons. And he got very defensive. He was like, 'You can't *just* buy these weapons.' But the fact is you can still buy them."

"Guns are terrible," said Susan.

And the rest of us agreed: guns are terrible. Fun, but terrible.

Pew pew

It's a tool. It's a weapon. It's a piece of sports equipment. It's a fetish. It's a plot device. It's a game mechanic. It's a power-up. It's a nightmare. It's a Christmas present. It's a voting issue. It's a right. It's a responsibility. It's a plague. It's death. It's rated PG-13. The gun is a monolith. It claims the lives of schoolchildren, and soldiers, and people of colour unfortunate enough to encounter a trigger-happy cop.

A tangle of symbols and history and emotion and politics—the gun is a load-bearing symbol in our society. Video games, movies, TV, and entire genres of literature depend on the gun in its most abstract and non-lethal capacities. Even real-life gun violence is filtered through the warping devices of narrative and news before it reaches the average viewer. Iconic and ubiquitous. Yet many people will never see a real gun fired in their entire lives, and certainly not into a warm human body.

Firearms advocates are quick to label their favourite weapons as tools. Morbidly accurate. A handgun feels like a cordless drill, only lighter in the butt, where the battery pack would be. But they are so much more than practical instruments. Thrilling plot devices, controversial murder machines, tingle-inducing ASMR aids, the central image of countless recurring nightmares. Cradling loaded guns and sighting my targets at the firing range, they felt disturbingly light.

When Dad's shooter revealed his blue pistol, my first thought was, *I can't believe this guy is threatening us with a toy.* Having pulled a trigger dozens more times than the gunman, I can say with confidence I wasn't too far from the mark. With every shot fired, I wished the gun in my hands were heavier.

TETROMINOES

WHEN YOU CLOSE YOUR EYES, you see them falling. Seven shapes, each made of four blocks: the long *I*, the hooked *L* and *J*, the crooked *S* and *Z*, the symmetrical *T*, and the box *O*. *Tetris* dreams, that strange insomnia where you see tetrominoes falling and rotating behind your eyelids as they settle into perfect lines that vanish when filled in by a final square peg. When Alexey Pajitnov invented the game in 1984, behind the Iron Curtain, an infinite game was only theoretical—mathematicians suspected that if you played long enough, the game would drop too many *S*s and *Z*s, making rows impossible to clear, pushing the playing field up to the ceiling and terminating the round. Behind your eyes, though, when you're trying to rest, the falling pieces always seem to fit.

In your waking life, you see the pattern. Everything slots into perfect, compact rows. Researchers of the "*Tetris* effect" theorize it's a deeply instinctual mode of learning new spatial rules sets. And it's not confined to the planet's most famous puzzle game. Anyone who's played enough video games can tell you there are *Portal* dreams that redefine your colour and space associations, *Pokémon* dreams that fill your imagination with elemental comparison charts, *Metal Gear Solid 2* dreams that paint your mind's eye with a sliding inventory of tranq darts, C4 explosives, and sniper rifles. Experience something on a screen for long enough, and your body wants to translate it into corporeal knowledge. Take the abstract and embody it.

Our screens show us violence. TVs, computer monitors, phones, video billboards, entertainment consoles on the backs of airplane seats, information panels hanging over subway platforms displaying breaking news and service updates—they show us stories built around a core of conflict. Sometimes it's highly contextual, like *Uncharted 2*'s Nathan Drake leaping between cars on a runaway train before shooting a Russian mercenary in the face with a shotgun and quipping, "Ouch." Other times it's completely abstract, like a line of blocks obliterating in a dopamine-producing explosion. In Anne Bogart's essay on violence in *A Director Prepares*, she posits that simply imposing a set of limitations on a situation, like giving an actor lines or telling her where to stand in a scene, is itself violence. Direction fences off freedom, and a performer pushes against her borders to create electrifying expression. That conflict between what an actor must do according to a script and her genuine human expression is the essential foundation of violence in media. The fact that the scripts demand so much gunplay is just a coincidence that elevates the violent core.

Still, the violence you see on screens is not like the violence you experienced first-hand—that horrible traumatic stuff you see when you close your eyes, but haven't played enough games to push the intrusive thoughts behind a curtain of fake falling blocks. That disconnect between presented reality and your memory alienates you, and in your loneliness you search for representation in entertainment, among the casual killing, the funny killing, the disgusting killing, the sad killing, the deadly torture, the coercive torture, the kind of killing you know is necessary but done with regret, the kind of killing directors are obligated to put in certain types of movies and shows to make them viable at the box office, the kind of killing your teachers said God forgave because your grandparents didn't have a choice but to fight in a war.

It only takes a minute and the right keywords to find an anonymous image board on the internet where users post pictures of gore. It feels much more real than the violence of film, TV, books, and games. Not because there is a chance it actually happened, but because it's divorced from the imposed meaning of narrative. Zero context. Just post after post of fucked-up data, coalescing in patterns of light on the screen, glowing in the shape of limp bodies dangling from rafters, the obliterated limbs of landmine victims, fragments of real human bone, blank eyes in pale faces. Animated gifs of silhouettes falling great distances, like tetrominoes.

Sven knows about the gore boards. The two of you talk about them as you sit on the floor of your apartment, eating pizza, listening to records, and playing chess after a long shift of telemarketing.

"Peter, I have to stop. I'm getting addicted to these pics and it can't be good."

"Same." But you're pretty sure he's exaggerating. There's a grin in his voice that betrays hidden awe. You've heard this smile before, when he described meeting a girlfriend's father who was a plastic surgeon specializing in reconstructive procedures. After eating dinner at the doctor's house, he showed Sven a slideshow presentation of his work on military personnel maimed by roadside bombs in Afghanistan. The repairing of brutality. Like seeing the gore board gifs in reverse, or starting a new game of *Tetris*. You're secretly jealous.

Chess and gore are perfectly paired obsessions. Violence on different levels of abstraction, unlimited in supply and codified enough to affect your dreams. You can split your computer screen down the middle, with one side playing instructional chess videos and the other refreshing the latest visceral posts from an anonymous legion of digital grave robbers. A JPEG of a naked corpse and a YouTube video about the Sicilian Defence narrated by Kevin from TheChessWebsite.com. Testimony from a sarin gas attack survivor and an endgame puzzle from *Bobby Fischer Teaches Chess*. Abstraction. Symbols. The representation of conflict. Keep playing the game with Sven and the repetition works its hallucinatory magic. New tetrominoes, same playing field.

You close your eyes at night and you see the chessboard. You picture the grid, visualize the movements, memorize the tactics. You feel the clicking-into-place satisfaction of a bishop pinning a knight to its king, like pulling back the hammer on a .38 calibre snub nose, the one you used to dream of, blue like the *Tetris J*. Your intrusive post-traumatic nighttime thoughts have been replaced by phantom game pieces, along with the cruise dreams and the father-dying-in-your-arms dreams. Compared to the *Tetris* effect, your violent memories start to look like rule sets of their own, running through your body's primal game-learning engine, teaching you how to do better next time. Press *Start* to continue. Insert coins. Get mugged by an arcade cabinet to sleep better. Sit on the floor with Sven, look down on your pretend wars. This can be the new violence, nothing like the old violence.

Desensitization is the word that comes to mind. But you're not some battle-hardened warrior—you're a twenty-something chess enthusiast who doesn't flinch at videos of people giving themselves paper cuts between their fingers. Close enough to the screen to understand that you're nowhere near the explosions, you see the little coloured dots that comprise each image, and you perform your role as an audience member, as a searcher, as a survivor. Eventually, you become an expert. You watch it all, over and over, intellectualize it, overstate the verisimilitude of a culture devoid of memory, pain, fear, and adrenalin. You internalize the rules, turn the game into work. Writing about media is easy, like keeping a dream journal for a job. You watch and rewatch, you analyze, you write, you publish, you get paid. Close your eyes and see the human mandala in *Hannibal*, the beer can men in *True Detective*, the castration and flaying of Theon Greyjoy in *Game of Thrones*.

This is the shared experience, so it feels more real than your own private traumatic event. Dad got shot, you felt his blood, and no one can relate to that. It wasn't on a screen.

Not like the violence you discuss with TV series celebrities during your side hustle as a media critic. On the phone, in fancy hotel rooms, on the red carpet, you connect the screen to reality, pushing your face flat against the liquid crystals of culture and feeling the warmth on your cheek.

In a Shangri-La guest suite, you ask Taylor Schilling if *Orange Is the New Black* gave her a new appreciation for the struggles of prison inmates. Famke Janssen sips tea as she emphasizes how much she hates gore, despite having to rip the heart out of her co-star in season 2 of *Hemlock Grove*. On the phone, you ask Nick Frost about how much training he had to do to learn his stunts for *Into the Badlands*. Not much, it turns out—he used to do tae kwon do, but had to take a break when acting took off because visible bruises interfere with the casting process. When he says your name, his voice brings you in. *Tetris* dream to *Tetris* reality. What they do, what you have done, it's all a spectrum of story. When your traumatic memories bubble up, you naturally mix your pain with the media, fit it into a row of blocks and watch it disappear, giving you room to breathe. You can live here on this plane of shared imagination. A list of high scores next to familiar names.

And one day, you watch an episode of the *Breaking Bad* prequel *Better Call Saul*. Morally backsliding criminal lawyer Jimmy McGill has recently been traumatized from witnessing extreme gun violence, and he asks reluctant contract killer Mike Ehrmantraut, "When will this be over for me?" Mike tells Jimmy he will be haunted for a very long time, until one day he will realize he hasn't thought about it for a while. Then he will learn he is capable of forgetting. But

Mike's solution is a paradox, and the implication tears you apart. Acknowledging the absence of your pain invites it back in. And then, as if recognizing a terrible chess blunder one move too late, your stomach will drop and you will be thinking about it: the real stuff, the physical stuff, the personal, unshareable stuff. And the pieces will fall faster, imperfectly. You don't know where it fits. A glitch in your video game. All *Z*s and *S*s, piling up, leaving gaps. The music speeds up. The rows stack high. And you're back where you started.

HOW TO RESTORE A TIMELINE

A RED LINE STRETCHING through infinite black space. It's a thread where there should be a tapestry—my synesthetic sense of time. But it's been like this for years. Out here, in the intergalactic space of post-traumatic life, time is cold and flavourless. If I look back to the early days of the millennium, or further on to the 1990s, a rich landscape of memory spans out in a fluid spectrum of green, yellow, blue, purple, silver, gold, white. Even grey and brown seem brilliant compared to the emptiness of today. Between the vibrancy of then and the void of now lies an obstruction. A blockage. A giant red dot. Sickly and pulsing. Never diminishing. A crimson circle from which time's current minuscule thread emerges. When I picture it in my mind, it's the size of a thousand suns. But when I feel the occlusion, as a knot of nausea deep in my body's core, I understand it as a vacuous singularity. In order to talk about these kinds of things in therapy and in writing, they need names. I call this red dot the nucleus.

The nucleus feels like a scar that cracks open anew whenever I think about Dad's shooting. It feels conspiratorial, like some evil geometry from the pages of Junji Ito. This dot hates me. If I gaze deep enough into it with my mind's eye, meditating as I was taught in theatre school and cognitive behavioural therapy, I can see the silhouette of a revolver and the dark skeleton outline of Limon. The shooter is there. The gun. All my worst memories collapsed with enough gravity to emit an event horizon. This nucleus disrupts my timeline, and I'm so fucking tired of living in its singular light.

"THAT CLOCK IS NOT YOUR FRIEND," said the Man in the Blue Gi. He caught me glancing at it as I ran between testing stations on the grey dojo mats. The grading was about seventy-five minutes into its two-day run-time, and while my body was in screaming pain from the push-ups and the squats and the drills, I felt that he was wrong. Its constant ticking promised an end to the pain, when my legs felt like giving way. Or when I was dry heaving into the garbage can. Every rotation of the red second hand was a victory. One moment closer to my black belt.

The other black belt candidates and I were sitting in horse stances, performing blocks and punches. Our senior students, a retinue of instructors, and Shihan himself scrutinized every detail. They threw punches for us to deflect and tested the stability of our footwork with firm shoves. The Man in the Blue Gi left the mats with a bow, entered the storage closet near the drinking fountain, and took out a stepladder. He bowed again as he stepped back onto the training area, unfolded the ladder, climbed two steps, grabbed the clock, and took it some place deep in the studio. It might as well have been on the moon. We were training outside of time. The burning seemed endless. And that's when the screaming started.

THERE'S NO ROOM FOR ironic distance in a scream. It's primal. It comes from that amorphous core where pure emotion resides. Flex your abdominal muscles and firmly chop the area under your ribs—you will feel the nerves outline its shape. This reservoir houses my nucleus of pain and memory. The ambient, bone-warping gravity of anxiety and depression. The image of a blue gun. The red tangle of thread, balled up and metastasized. It used to be a timeline. The nucleus pulses. It bleeds. And if I need to push myself further, if I need to vent my energy, I can split it open and release a runaway sun. Scream. Scream in harmony with the cosmic resonance of that evil red dot.

The kiai is what outsiders laugh at when they see martial arts in action—the powerful shout of the karate-ka. It's the most difficult aspect of training for new students. They are self-conscious. Screaming isn't normally allowed. It's impolite, aggressive, and violent. But more important, a true scream is vulnerable. That is where it gets its power. To scream a kiai in a reverse punch is to commit fully to the action. Pivot in your stance, shifting your entire body so that your back leg and your hips coordinate with your two front knuckles, and allow that perfect alignment to act as a conduit for that nuclear blast. Scream in full support of your action, and only then can you really call it a punch.

There's no doubt in a scream. No second guessing. We scream in agony. We scream in anticipation. We scream in despair. We scream in jubilation. We scream with laughter, but never critically. Irony is obliterated in the moment of expression. There is no distance between the mind and body when we open the chamber to our nuclei and vocalize our catharsis. It's transformation, signalled with a sonic blast. It's the genuine you.

MY FRIENDS, A HANDFUL of rock music and comedy nerds, had little patience for songs that screamed about their feelings, so I hid my Linkin Park *Meteora* box set when they came over. I loved the music on Linkin Park's sophomore effort dearly. But it had a stigma, so I slipped the CD case into the top-left drawer of the wooden desk next to my bed.

I listened to Linkin Park alone as I did homework or read fantasy novels or chatted with my friends on MSN Messenger. I did not talk about it. The band's screaming rap-rock tunes about mental illness and addiction and self-harm were direct, emotional, and as vulnerable as they were aggressive. In the early days, singer Chester Bennington and rapper Mike Shinoda didn't even swear. They just emoted from a place of loud sincerity, spitting lyrics that spoke directly to teens like me with mood disorders.

The instinct to hide my enjoyment of Linkin Park feels the same as mental illness stigma. Songs like "Somewhere I Belong" and "Numb" and "Crawling" expressed emotions I felt at my most raw and vulnerable, and sometimes at my most dangerous to myself. Chester's scream became my scream, a surrogate vent for the pain of strong emotions I had nowhere to hide. When I was seventeen, I had bipolar II and listened to Linkin Park. Even under the umbrella of doctor-patient confidentiality, I only revealed one of those shameful identities.

In July 2017, Chester Bennington was found dead by suicide in his California home. That's when I decided to stop hiding my love of his music. It felt like a cosmic call to action. The man who provided relief to people with deadly emotions succumbed to his own. After a decade of living with my nucleus, I came to see Bennington as a brother in arms. Someone at war with his own radioactive core. It claimed him, the singer I looked to as a champion, and I worried it could happen to me. I needed a proactive way to fight the gravity. Maybe the secret was in the scream.

The aspect of his death that disturbed me most involved the Stone Temple Pilots. No one loved STP more than Chester. In 2001, he told *Revolver*, "Stone Temple Pilots is the best band that's ever existed in the history of the world, I don't care what anybody says." And he believed it. "I think ten, twenty years from now, you're going to be hearing a new STP album, and going, 'It's another good one!'"

In a March 2002 interview with *Rolling Stone*'s David Fricke, Bennington revealed even more about his fandom. Prior to the release of Linkin Park's 2000 debut album, *Hybrid Theory*, Chester saw a double platinum Stone Temple Pilots record on the wall of Warner Brothers promotions manager Myra Simpson. He geeked out and she told him, "If you go gold by Christmas, I'll give it to you." Miraculously,

Hybrid Theory sold over a half-million copies by December, and from then on the singer slept with the STP plaque on his Linkin Park tour bus.

In 2013, after Linkin Park established itself as a global sensation, STP fired its walking disaster of a frontman Scott Weiland and hired Chester as their new singer. Bennington had achieved his ultimate dream. He became the peer of his heroes. But that scale of achievement wanes. It doesn't last like the bad stuff. The cutting and strangling stuff, the crying and writhing stuff. The glowing nuclei in our cores, absorbing negativity like a black hole and gaining mass. That's the problem. Nothing persists like our pain. Not even our greatest accomplishments. Getting your black belt, singing with your favourite band. They aren't enough to save us from our darkest impulses.

Chester's most beautiful songs are from his last album with Linkin Park, *One More Light*. The screaming is sparse on this one, replaced by earnest, clear-voiced singing. He communicates some of the most direct depictions of mental health anguish through his lyrics and traces a path of hope out of the darkness. In the title track he coos about the ephemeral nature of good things. In the first radio single, "Heavy," he belts about the unbearable weight of his problems, and how he could be free if only he could let go.

We would be better off if the good parts of life left lasting marks. But we don't even have words for these things. Can we be haunted by our accomplishments? Pride is a deadly sin. Nostalgia is nothing but dissatisfaction. I'm writing this with tears in my eyes, because I know in my heart that if we could find a way to make our best memories last like trauma does—create some sort of good, positive version of a scar—we can outrun the gravity of our nuclei.

I WAS THIRTY THE first time I sparred with a stranger after developing PTSD. Eleven years after Dad was shot, which means it was ten years after I last stepped foot in Shihan's dojo. I lived in Halifax, and Emma and I decided to learn tae kwon do from a local grandmaster who won bronze at the Barcelona Olympics. My history with karate was something I left behind in my pre-traumatic life. A faded accomplishment. I was more comfortable with a different martial art. It meant I could start over.

Emma and I climbed the ranks quickly, our belt colours flitting through their rainbow of ascension. When I was a green belt, I entered into a sparring tournament in Antigonish on Grandmaster's recommendation. There are few adult colour belt divisions in sparring. It was just me and a yellow belt from another school. He was shorter than me, older. And I was no slouch. My previous experience in karate sometimes got me into trouble—some karate moves are illegal in the tae kwon do ring—but it made me comfortable on the mats. The difference in rank alone was enough for me to feel confident in my chances.

We squared off. We bowed. We touched gloves. The referee started the match with a shout and my opponent began screaming, launching a flurry of roundhouse kicks. I blocked one. I blocked another. But the third hit home on my chest pad. The impact launched my mind into the past. I was no longer in the high school gym. The rush of waves crashing on the shore, the humidity. Wooden boards under my feet. But instead of a gunman it was this yellow belt. Kicking me. The buzzer sounded. Round one was over and my nightmare was just starting.

The final score was an embarrassing washout. My ringside coach, who Grandmaster's wife once said looked like Jesus Christ, helped me keep enough focus to land a few defensive back kicks, proving I wasn't completely useless. But my defeat echoed. In the days after the tae kwon do tournament, I felt my bones straining like they did when I was nineteen and freshly traumatized. At night I dreamed the old dreams about the pier, the gun, the blood, the labyrinthine halls of the *Liberty*. I practically forgot the incident that started this fresh round of flashbacks and hypervigilance, my symptoms so intense they overwrote the "I lost a martial arts tournament" narrative with "I saw my father crumple at the impact of a bullet."

I didn't stop training. Going to the tae kwon do studio helped soothe the symptoms. Physical strain and the lactic acid ache of workout recovery calmed the nucleus. And martial arts studios are one of the only places where you can go to scream, punctuating your attacks with bursts of sincerity.

A year after those flashbacks, the training accumulated. I signed up for the annual black belt test and entered into a new state of candidacy, committing to months of higher-level training in service to a public grading scheduled for December. The tae kwon do grading was not the secret society initiation I knew from karate. The two arts are fundamentally different, like comparing a volcano to a tornado.

But the core principles were close enough. The ascension. The community. The physical transformation that occurs after doing thousands of push-ups in just a few months.

The tae kwon do black belt test culminated with a demonstration of dynamic power: punching through a concrete block. On the day of the final assessment, after we'd proven ourselves in fitness, self-defence, sparring, and forms, we sat in a line at the edge of the mats. One by one we stood before Grandmaster. We bowed and squared off with a thick slab of cement held up by cinder blocks, looking like a brutalist shrine to the colour grey.

Exhausted beyond belief, strained in some places, bruised in others. A knuckle on my left hand was already bleeding from punching through wooden boards earlier in the day. I bowed to Grandmaster and took in my opponent. Rough, impenetrable. In that moment I was fully present. No thoughts of the past, no worries of the future. Just me and the block. I chambered my right hand, readying a strike, and committed myself fully to the punch. I screamed, the shrine collapsed into a pile of cement pieces and dust. A faint flicker. For a moment I could see colour in my timeline again.

THREE MONTHS AFTER RECEIVING my new black belt, we were in lockdown. The coronavirus took away my connection to the bright past, and my martial arts achievement dulled with every new wave of infections. Buried under the stress of adapting to a new state of being, in which the community of an indoor sport could mean certain death for some, I fell back into the colourless state. A red thread stretching through black void. No future from a tangled past.

Bright spots still popped up. Moments with Emma, with Nick, with my parents. New communities rekindled online in the boredom of dark isolated winters. But I never went back to the dojang. A second black belt, next to my first one, in the bottom drawer of my bedroom dresser. Massive achievements are so easy to lose sight of because they don't hurt like trauma. And there is always more trauma, which conspires with the pain that preceded it, dragging it forward and building upon its mass. Making it feel fresh.

Each new existential wound compares itself to the landscape of slights that make up our personal histories. How bad is this, really, compared to what you've already been through? How bad can it get? But the trick is: it doesn't matter. Misfortune isn't in competition with itself. It groups together and tangles, collapsing into the singularity you can feel in your core, expanding its event horizon. There is no sense of linear time in a black hole. Maybe that's why trauma fucked up my synesthesia. The clock isn't your friend.

My nucleus bulked up as the pandemic turned life into a conveyor belt of disaster and despair. It feasted on the deaths of friends and the pain of family members. Sickness, recession, climate disaster, and political strife set the stage for Mom's cancer diagnosis. Then my friend Amelia's. I couldn't remember anything good anymore. The block I broke was nothing but a memory while my trauma oozed fresh.

I'D LOST FRIENDS BEFORE. Josh. Andrew. Maura. I'd lost family members. All my grandparents, my infant cousin. And then I was tuning into Amelia's funeral through a webcam to hear the eulogy for a thirty-two-year-old shining star who blinked out of existence. My memories of Amelia joined the memorial deep in the core.

I worried about Mom. I tried to remain positive. Because of what happened with Dad all those years ago, I felt an urge to fight against any harm that would threaten my family, but I couldn't be with her for her sixteen weeks of chemotherapy. It's irrational and ridiculous. I'm a writer; I don't have a cancer cure. But on a deep, bone-marrow level, I see encroaching death and long to perform marathon feats of strength, if not to fight it off then in solidarity with its victims.

"You know what this reminds me of, strangely enough?" I asked Mom during our weekly phone call. "The black belt grading."

The year after I left for school, Mom did her own test. A four-month gauntlet of intense training, capped with a surreal two-day assessment. Now she was facing another sixteen weeks of endurance.

As true as it was, I was also projecting. I compared Mom's chemo to the black belt grading because I wanted to be in control. I wanted to cheer her on. I wanted to know fate could be defeated with feet and fists. If my nucleus grew any more, I worried the gravity would cause me to implode.

After I hung up the phone, I dug into my office closet and pulled out a grey-green shoebox. Inside, among a lifetime's worth of souvenirs, I picked out a silver disc with the word "brown-stripe" Sharpied on the front. The DVD of karate lessons Shihan burned for me before I left the dojo for theatre school. I dropped it into the tray of my desktop computer and the tower hummed. I saw the dojo. The grey mats and mirrors. The face of my mentor. He walked through the motions I once knew so well. The katas and self-defences that work best when you scream. I felt the power of those memories and a need to revisit them.

I shut down my computer. I laced up my running shoes. I downloaded a Linkin Park playlist onto my phone. And I started running again.

THE CLOCK IS NOT your friend. But if you need that push over the edge into screaming release, it can be a tool. It can keep you accelerating. It can keep you honest. But it won't tell you when it's going to end. That's not how this works.

I run in the mornings. I run in the heat and the cold and the fog and the rain. I run in the blinding sun. I hit the button on my stopwatch and see the liquid crystals pour out milliseconds into a black puddle of numbers. Accumulation. Time drowning the present, covering the past like scar tissue.

The watch reminds me I've been here before. Starting from my driveway, I run up the hill to the main road and make my way alongside the morning commuter traffic heading to the bridge that traverses the harbour. When I get to the mailbox, I glance at my wrist. Anything over eighty seconds prompts me to speed up in order to stay on pace. It's a good time for it because I turn right and run downhill toward the navy base before taking a sharp left on the road that passes under the bridge. I follow that road downtown, and it takes me to a parkette with a daffodil garden that looks out at the mouth of the harbour into the Atlantic Ocean. I touch the park's sign, then turn around and run home, taking a route closer to the water's edge.

Every pang of doubt, all the pain in my muscles begging me to stop, they are answered with a glance at the time. Acceleration is the goal. Run faster than before. Push the bar higher for your future self. Remember who you used to be, how fast you ran back then. Push against stasis and understand the pain as keeping something positive alive. Because when you push against your limits you embody the pure sincerity of a scream. That place of zero irony. It's not self-harm, but it's close. It's the good version.

Running is a state of active meditation. By setting my body in motion I honour all the other circuits I ran. When I drive forward and improve my time, I hold two opposing thoughts in my mind. My track is a circle, from my drive- way to the daffodils and back. My track is a straight line, unbroken, through time and space.

Running around my brown-brick elementary school for cross-country tryouts. Sprinting on the rubberized track during high school gym class. Forty runs for black belt, around the map Shihan drew, and more running on his rural property. Running back to get the shoe that fell from Dad's foot when I dragged him off the pier. I would have sprinted the rest of the way to the ship if I could, but settled for hobbling through Limon instead. Treadmills afterward, which I jacked up to high speed in a game of chicken with myself, thinking about Costa Rica. Self-flagellation through human locomotion. Running around Toronto parks and the Halifax Common and the padded tae kwon do studio. And now this: running to the park with the yellow flowers, where the ocean bleeds into the sky.

On most summer days I can see a cruise ship docked at the mouth of the harbour. A white blemish on blue. The *Liberty* had a running track on the Panorama Deck, above the Lido. That's where Nick and I smoked together for the first time, the night we saw our father's blood. Most ships have tracks. If I could see them from my vantage point, I'd give a runner's wave. One of those three-finger salutes that come with a nod of allyship—we're running alone, but we're in this together. The ecstasy, the grief, the burn of ascension.

All the colours of all those memories are connected to the forever run, which started before the timeline tangled and diminished. When I push myself to get to the mailbox a second quicker, when I refuse to listen to the parts of my body that want to slow down or rest, the green, the gold, the blue, the white, purple, orange, pink, and red—colours I used to associate with the present and future but that are now stuck before the tangle—they bleed out of my activated core, painting this moment of internal screaming with a new kind of mark. Not a scar. Not a disability. A personal tradition of continuing forward, trailing psychic rainbow graffiti on the streets, across the sky, reflecting off the water.

Treat the good memories like the bad ones. Obsess over them, associate them with the sincerity of a scream. And don't stop. A lifetime ago, in the cold golden and burgundy part of my timeline, I was sitting in front of a bonfire. Shihan was there. He told me and my fellow newly minted black belts that life would present us with impossible battles. But impossible battles are worth fighting. So I choose to honour the memory of that moment. I hold it with the importance of my trauma and refuse to let it fade. I run faster. I run farther. I rage against the temporal void where I once saw a rich band of vibrant light. And if the nucleus defeats me, it will be in battle. You will find my scarred remains at the end of a brilliant trail of colour.

JUPITER

WE KNOW JUPITER FROM a distance. Orbiting 778 million kilometres from our sun, the massive planet is more than twice as big as the others in our solar system combined. That's what makes it so easy to spot. Look up on a clear night and find the dot of light that doesn't twinkle. Higher in the sky than Venus, and deeper into the night. If you're unsure, look through a pair of binoculars. See four pinpricks aligned across its axis and you've got the right one. Those miniscule dots of light are the Galilean moons: Io, Europa, Ganymede, and Callisto. The astronomer Galileo mapped their movements in 1610, discovering that their positions around the gas giant can be used as a chronometer. Jupiter tells time.

Humans have sent nine spacecraft to explore the Jovian system. We know the planet takes twelve Earth years to orbit the sun, but its day is less than half as long as ours. Jupiter has seventy-five known moons, including the four bright ones Galileo found, some of which have the ingredients to support life. It is composed of swirling bands of stormy vapour, providing the orb with its iconic marble aspect: stripes of stormy orange and white with a big red dot—the eye of Jupiter—an ancient hurricane twice the size of Earth. The dark side of Jupiter receives moonlight from its satellites. In 2017, the Juno spacecraft photographed lightning strikes, the images of which evoke distant nocturnal thunder.

The name Jupiter literally means "sky father." Personified as a god, he is the Roman Jove, a jealous and spiteful king known to wreak destruction on the mortal realm. The metaphor lines up with the planet's history. Formed before the other planets, it received our solar system's first dawn. As for its temperament, researchers believe that five billion years ago, Jupiter migrated closer to the sun, its gravity flinging ninety percent of planet-making material from our inner solar system into our young star's blazing inferno. All that remained after the cosmic tantrum was enough for four small terrestrial worlds, including our own. But look at Jupiter another way and you'll see a nurturing force.

It's said that two ingredients are needed for life to flourish: time and stability. As a cosmic defender and a natural chronometer, Jupiter provides both. It protects us from the phenomena that might otherwise disrupt the chain of evolution, keeping the civilization-killing rocks in the asteroid belt where they belong and absorbing other celestial objects of mass death. Objects like Shoemaker-Levy 9, the comet that Jupiter tore apart with its tidal forces before a fragment pierced its clouds like a bullet. The resulting impact was visible from Earth as a black scar. Photographs documenting

Jupiter's wound before it healed remind us that we don't have to face the cold violence of space on our own.

THE MOON WAS OUT, hanging over the bay. Not great conditions for stargazing, given the lunar light dampening the night sky's fidelity. But Nick and I decided to take the Bushnell telescope from our parents' living room onto the deck anyway to see if we could find the *Apollo* landing site. We didn't know if that was possible. We'd never tried before. Referencing a map on Nick's phone, we found the area where human boots had touched moon dust. Not that we could see evidence of humanity. Just white rocks defined by their shadows. High on a sense of cosmic excitement, we searched for other shining lights to explore. Pivoting our scope away from the glaring Sea of Tranquility, we focused on another, smaller bright circle.

Adjusting the lenses, we centred the light and took turns marvelling. A marble in the sky, bisected by a clockwork of glinting dots. Tracking the moons with my eye, I thought of a thread, stretching through space, defined and dominated by the grand majesty of Jupiter, with its inescapable gravity and unmatched historical significance. Even with the enhanced magnification of the Bushnell, the planet looked tiny. The God-sized ball of violent storms seemed small enough that it could balance on the tip of my finger as long as I held my breath to keep it from blowing away.

I'd never really thought of Jupiter as a place. But there it was, watching over Earth as it had for billions of years. For the birth of our home and the formation of our moon. The extinction of the dinosaurs. The ice age. The evolution of human civilization with its colourful mosaic of love, anger, despair, and curiosity. Jupiter has been there my entire life, glowing in the sky, even if I didn't recognize it or appreciate its influence. Our shepherd in the void.

We have been conditioned to repeat popular existential concepts when talking about our fragile place in the universe. To go through the performance of angst and dread and ennui when we consider our insignificant lives in the big picture. Trillions upon trillions of galaxies give texture to the universe, each with countless stars and planets, and everything we know is confined to our pale-blue dot. Something as small as personal trauma disappears at that gargantuan scale. Basic human concepts like good and bad are lost in the grand ballet between nebulae and blue giants. A mote of dust in the presence of big bangs and super-massive black holes.

The first time Nick and I looked at a starry sky together, we stood on the deck of a cruise ship, the night after our father was shot through the middle. Opening our hearts as brothers, sharing our pain and disbelief, we found a moment of calm. I felt part of an elegant system. We must have seen Jupiter then, a bright light in the sky on the worst of all days, unrecognizable for our violent distractions.

ACKNOWLEDGEMENTS

THANK YOU TO LEIGH NASH, former publisher at House of Anansi, for believing in this book since its inception. Thank you to Andrew Faulkner, whose constant companionship, keen eye, and honesty helped me give form to abstract emotions—a true companion through the darkness. Thank you to Shivaun Hearne for bringing *How to Restore a Timeline* through its transformation from manuscript to essay collection, and for inspiring the inclusion of tarot imagery.

My undying gratitude goes to the entire team at House of Anansi, whose care, enthusiasm, and professionalism helped turn this deeply personal project into a Very Good Book. Jenny McWha, Emma Rhodes, Ingrid Wu, Laura Chapnick, Jessey Glibbery, Debby de Groot, Douglas Richmond, Karen Brochu—thank you. Greg Tabor, thank you for designing such a cool cover. Lucia Kim, thank you for carrying that coolness into the text.

This book is about my family, who graciously permit me to tell stories about them. Emma, my first reader, my co-dreamer. Nick, my closest friend, my twin snake. Mom, my role model, my fellow black belt. Dad, my hero. Thank you all for being supportive and open during the long process, not only of writing this book, but of learning to live happily after what we've been through. I know the future will only bring us closer.

Alex Perala and Susan Stover—thank you for another symposium. Séamus Gallagher—thank you for asking the deep questions about film and money. Mike Sholars—thank you for being my Otacon. If everyone had friends as open to new experiences and ideas as you, our world would be more peaceful.

I mention many mentors in these pages, all of whom taught me the lessons needed to write a book. Kevin Sealy taught me the value of modesty, perseverance, and indomitable spirit. Michael Greyeyes introduced me to creative viewpoints I apply in everything I create. Grandmaster Woo Yong Jung taught me how to kick again and break through new limits. Thank you all for your tutelage. I don't know who I'd be without you.

The memories at the heart of these essays come from times of terminal loneliness. Katie DuTemple, Andrea McCulloch, John McKinnon—thank you for your friendship when I needed it most. Many years ago, I tried to write the story of my trauma as a linear memoir. Dana Hopkins helped me learn to write about my experience of gun violence and articulate concepts like the nucleus. Thank you, Dee.

"Waiting for the Red Giant" was originally commissioned by All Lit Up in 2021. Thank you, Mandy Bayrami, for inspiring my first steps toward this second collection.

I am grateful for the creators of all the media discussed in these essays, but there are three who deserve special mention. Hideo Kojima creates art in a way that makes me excited to be alive. Carmen Maria Machado's memoir *In the Dream House* showed me the power of exploring trauma through experimental forms of nonfiction. Chuck Klosterman's writing taught me the difference between life, death, and criticism. Thank you.

Finally, I've been told never to thank the dead in print. But I lost a friend while writing this book. In the last two years of her life, she taught me the strength of hope, positivity, and colour. Amelia, I tried to make this one a little less scary so you could read it.

SOURCES

In the essay "Haunted Videotape," the quote from Walter Benjamin is from "On the Concept of History," thesis 9, 1942, translated by Lloyd Spencer, available through the Simon Fraser University website, care of Andrew Feenberg (sfu.ca/~andrewf/books/Concept_History_Benjamin.pdf).

In the essay "On Batman," the quote from George Orwell is from "The Art of Donald McGill," *Horizon*, September 1941, available through the Orwell Foundation (orwellfoundation .com/the-orwell-foundation/orwell/essays-and-other-works/ the-art-of-donald-mcgill/).

The epigraph to the essay "This Otaku Man Is Happy" is from the BBC News article "Why I 'Married' a Cartoon Character," August 17, 2019 (bbc.com/news/stories-49343280).

In the essay "Paul McCartney's Head in the Bardo," the

quote from Chögyam Trungpa Rinpoche is from *The Tibetan Book of the Dead: The Great Liberation through Hearing in the Bardo*, translated by Francesca Freemantle (Boulder, CO: Shambhala, 2019).

PETER COUNTER is a culture critic writing about television, video games, film, music, mental illness, horror, and technology. He is the author of *Be Scared of Everything: Horror Essays*, and his non-fiction has appeared in *The Walrus*, *All Lit Up*, *Motherboard*, *Art of the Title*, *Electric Literature*, and the anthology *Empty the Pews: Stories of Leaving the Church*. He lives in Dartmouth, Nova Scotia. Find more of his writing at peterbcounter.com and everythingisscary.com.